Through Tears
and Sugar Cubes

By L. G. Gibson

Dedication

This book is dedicated to my husband and best friend, Russell, and our children: Angela, Carrie, Chris, Rich, Kaila, Matthew, Russ Jr., Ricardo, and Johnny. Our family was woven together by God. Never think you were lost in the crowd. Every unique personality was needed for us to be who we are.

Russell, you have loved me and watched as God helped me bloom through all the adversity of my life. You sang, "You light up my life" to me on our wedding day, and you, dear husband, did just that for me.

Angela, you have picked up the sword of the Lord and pressed through.

Carrie, you flit about like a beautiful butterfly bringing smiles and love to everyone who knows you.

Chris, you are like a bear, strong and powerful, but the teddy bear in you causes all to be drawn to your gentle spirit.

Rich, your strength and Joseph-like quality will raise you above adversity to bless others.

Kaila, you are like sunshine. Let your rays touch us all. You warm our hearts.

Matthew, your love for God and gentleness mark the real strengths of a man. Preach, babe, preach!

Russ Jr., you shine the most as a husband and father. You look the tallest with your baby in your arms.

Ricardo, you are our Haiti miracle. God's plan is great for you and you are strong enough to achieve it.

Johnny, you are a gift and a light for the future. Let it shine for generations.

Through embracing you all and being loved by you all, this book has come forth.

I DEDICATE THIS BOOK TO YOU!

Acknowledgment

Thank you, Father God, for showing me just how much you love me and just how much you love us all.

God bless my parents who prayed for me during the difficult times even though they didn't know why life was so hard for me.

Thank you, Rich, for pressing through the first editing before I could show this book to anyone.

Thank you, Joy. You, my friend, have loved me with all my faults and spoken wisdom into my life.

Diana, you listened to that little girl in me and helped walk me through the dark and bring me to Truth.

My life-long friend Joyce has always encouraged me and helped pull this book out of me.

Linda, thank you for helping me find a way to camp as a kid. The Word I learned probably saved my life.

Special thanks to the ones who saw my vision and told me to run with it. My cheerleaders were Jan, Julie, Pastor Mark and Karen, and Debbie and Robert Paul. They always seemed to know what I needed. Thank you!

Table of Contents

Prologue

This book has been fifty-plus years in the making. It is not a story of sexual abuse, rather a book about overcoming the horrific trauma experienced by the victims.

News headlines are chock-full of accounts of kidnappings and abuse. Young girls are being locked up for decades and used as sex slaves. Many are sold like cattle to the highest bidder and flippantly passed from stall to stall. Children are stolen out of their beds in the middle of the night from their own homes and simultaneously robbed of the innocence of their childhood. Trusted friends and family defiantly take advantage of their authority and positions. Deceptive fathers and stepfathers violate innocence, and misguided brothers become predators. Some fall prey to the aggressions of a high school date or even a teacher. Casual sex among middle school children has become a game in many schools. They have no idea that with each encounter, they are blindly giving away a little part of themselves.

Unfortunately, child and sexual abuse statistics have steadily increased during my lifetime.

- A girl has a greater chance of being sexually abused than she has of being in a successful marriage.

- Every ninety-six seconds someone in the United States is sexually assaulted.

- Every eight minutes child protective services substantiates the evidence of child sexual abuse.

- Eighty-two percent of victims are female.

- The average age of a sex-trafficked victim is thirteen years old.

- Over 64 percent of all sexual abuse victims attempt or commit suicide.

- The estimated number of women who have become victims of rape since 1998 in the United States is 17,700,000.

The total amount of money rape costs victims (including sexual abuse) every year in the United States is $127 billion.

No matter how or when it happened, the damage is still the same, and all relive their torment over and over and over again. They are being held captive to emotional, mental, physical, and sexual abuse, often paralyzing them from becoming who they were created to be. They are living a life through dark-colored glasses, and although the external wounds heal, their internal wounds are either still bleeding or have been pushed down so far that darkness covers them.

Many times in my life I have shouted to myself, "I'm going to be all right! I am going to be all right! I *have* to be all right!" Those words would blast off of my tongue as a declaration not only for me, but for all of heaven and hell that needed to hear it. I knew that if I did not stand I would crumble into a million pieces. My heart was already shattered, and my mind was fragmented. Faith was the glue that held me together. I was not sure when or how, but I knew in my heart that God had a way to fix me. What I did not know was that He had a plan to make me "brand new."

The cry of my heart is to bring healing to numerous girls and women who have experienced any form of abuse. If you can read this book, you're not too young to receive from it. This book will guide you into a realm of healing you may not know exists, and it can give you hope beyond what you can imagine.

Your Creator has a better plan for your life than what you have experienced. If you knew there was a sure cure for cancer and you had the disease, wouldn't you run after it? Well, there is healing for your broken heart and your shattered mind. You can be set free from the shame and fear that holds you captive. You don't have to see those sickening images in your mind the rest of your life.

Throughout this book, I will share what I, and countless others, have experienced and provide you with an array of support and avenues for healing. If you are not a victim yourself, this book can certainly help a friend or family member.

Freedom is at your fingertips!

You will never be the same!

What do you have to lose?

Chapter One

GOOD GIRLS DON'T CRY

What does it mean to be a good girl? Good girls make their moms and dads happy. Good girls get smiles and surprises. You are loved if you're a good girl. A good girl can be proud of herself. *Good girls don't cry.*

I was brought up during a time when children obeyed grown-ups without question. If your mom or dad asked something of you, you were quick to respond. It wasn't hard to obey my parents because I loved them. You also obeyed any adult who was around you, whether they were family or not.

Our family was from the South, which also meant you were taught good manners. Children speak only when they are spoken to. Little girls smile a lot and only get slightly dirty. They play with dolls and tea sets and watch their grandmothers make bread. I was one such girl. We were from a small college town in North Carolina. It was a beautiful community where everyone knew each other. The streets were lined with beautiful, old oak trees. The buildings stood strong and majestic. Churches were on every block. Both sets of my grandparents lived in that same town. One lived on the north side and the other lived on the south side.

I was the middle child growing up between an older and a younger brother. As small children, my two brothers and I would walk from one house to the other to visit our grandparents. I loved to go with them to take walks. We felt all grown up as we walked together. We would stroll down the sidewalk and pass the local Esso gas station at the first corner. Just outside the front door stood a shiny, red and white Coke machine. Back then, a nickel would buy a cold bottle of soda to enjoy on what seemed to be a long walk to us.

We would walk right through town passing a soda shop and dime store and then stop by the post office to pick up our grandparents' mail. Even the postmaster knew us by name. He would always ask about our parents and grandparents. As we walked, friends and neighbors would wave. Occasionally, we would stop and sip a glass of water or eat a cookie offered along the way. It was a time, in that small town, when a child was everyone's responsibility. My dad's father worked at the local college for many years and my mom's mother managed the elementary school cafeteria. She knew every child in town.

We seemed like big stuff, walking down the sidewalk in expectation of a yummy treat at Grandma's house. My mom told me that as children we were nicknamed "the cookie kids." I can only smile when I remember those days.

When I was almost three years old we moved to the suburbs outside of Philadelphia, but we still spent holidays and three months of every summer in our hometown in North Carolina. As I write today, I realize that town was a refuge for me.

My early memories in Pennsylvania are of snow drifts and sled rides. We had snowball fights with neighborhood children and built snow caves in the drifts, filling them with snowballs. I remember sledding down a big hill near our home. I was still too young to go to school, but I went down that big hill sitting between my mother's legs or hanging on her back. Sometimes my dad would hold me tight and take me down that hill with him. Everyone in the neighborhood would come to that hill to sled in the evenings. When the sun began to set, and the snow would freeze again, our clothes would not get wet, so we could sled for hours. A large metal drum contained a fire that kept us all warm.

Our North Carolina town never had such wonderful snow. When we were too tired or too cold to hang onto our sleds anymore, we would make our way back to our small but cozy home. My mom would warm our hands and feet by rubbing them gently. She also prepared hot cocoa and cookies for us.

My mom was a beautiful southern belle with a knack for making biscuits and the gift of hospitality. She was one of many stay-at-home moms in our neighborhood. Our home was open to neighbors and friends and that was good, as our family was several hundred miles away.

Our neighborhood stood on a hilltop that overlooked a train track. Several of our neighbors became familiar with the sharp whistle of the train that blew each day as it passed. I remember a chain-link fence surrounding the hilltop which I am sure was placed there to ensure that little folks like me never fell near that track. The ground trembled when the train went by and it was a long way down. I felt scared when I stood beside that fence.

As a little child, it was a wonderful experience to watch trains go by day after day. Sometimes the conductor or the man in the shiny, red caboose would wave at us. We watched with excited little eyes, hoping to see someone. We imagined that after a while, they were looking for us, just like we were looking for them.

While we waited for the train we talked to the other moms and children, eagerly focusing on that track. One day a balding, elderly gentleman came by and joined us. He said he had once worked for the railroad. He was a wealth

4

of information about where that train came from and where it was going. It may all seem silly now, gathering to watch a train.

The older children even took time to count the cars out loud. That noisy train was a big deal and sometimes our "railroad man" friend would hold me up to get a better look. He said to just call him "Uncle." There were no other relatives around, so that seemed just fine.

In those days we didn't have an abundance of children's shows on television. Our days were mostly spent playing outside building forts and taking walks. Our imagination would run wild with us. We stayed in our own little neighborhood and felt safe there. There were plenty of adults around to protect us.

Uncle befriended my parents who were still in their twenties. He was a widower and to my sweet parents, that meant he needed a home-cooked meal from time to time and some extra TLC. He soon became an extra grandfather figure around our house. He even took us fishing with him, just as our real grandpa did. He was retired but he spent some of his time working as a janitor at a local church. My parents trusted him completely. They were good, loving parents and had no hint that a child predator was so close by. They had no way to discern the evil that they had allowed into their home.

My parents settled into their jobs and church and made many new friends. Uncle was right there to help them anytime a babysitter was needed. My mom was in a bowling league (and was very good, I must say). There was also a young married couples group that met at our church. These things offered parents a little time away from their children. Uncle was always willing to lend a hand. There were times when my older brother went off to school, and my mom had some type of an appointment, and my little brother and I would stay in his care.

My parents had absolutely no idea what this man was doing to their little princess. I was only three years old when it began, and it would not stop until we moved back to North Carolina seven years later. I will not go into the details as to what happened to me. It took me thirty years to get those images out of my mind; I will not paint them on the canvas of yours. I will say that, at times, it was no less than torture. Many times, I heard "Shhhh. Good girls don't cry." The fear that gripped me all those years kept his secret safe.

One thing that I have found for sure is that the enemy uses the same lies again and again. The torture is multiplied over and over with each new victim. Sexual abuse is a hideous crime.

I first shared some wonderful days and beautiful snow-filled evenings. Those were the times I needed to remember so that I would not drown in the sorrow of the darkness Uncle perpetrated upon me.

I will now relate the effects of my experience and how I became gloriously set free from each one. For example, when I step into the kitchen and pull out my grandma's "Pecan Crispy" cookie recipe, you can be assured that if I follow the recipe line by line I won't end up with a meatloaf. Rather, I will have baked the most delicious taste of heaven, and their aroma will take me back to the very kitchen where she baked them. I can even see her sweet smile. God put a recipe for your healing in His Word, and if you follow it, you will be healed! You will be made whole. I am thankful the Holy Spirit led me to this place of healing. I will share with you the stories of desperation that led to my cry for truth. I am so glad that the Holy Spirit has the answers.

My daughter suggested I share my grandmother's recipe with you. She lived in one of those beautiful, old houses in town with huge pecans trees in her backyard. I would help pick up those pecans and she would bake her delightful cookies for me. I will call them "Minnie's Pecan Crispy Cookies." The recipe is on page 126. I hope they will warm your belly as well as your heart.

Chapter Two

LET THE LIES BEGIN

My abuse started when I was so young that I can't even remember a time in my childhood when the memory wasn't there. Abused children are taught to deceive and lie. How else could they hide the secret? You are told, "Don't tell your mama," "Act like everything's all right," "You aren't really hurt," "No one is going to care," and "They won't believe you anyway." Lies become a deep well inside of us. We lie to cover up more lies. You learn to live in a world that isn't real. Some children have become so lost in that pretend world that they are never able to come back. The very people who could save us are the ones at whom the lies are directed.

My abuser told me, over and over, that he loved me and that I was "special." His wife had been dead for many years. He told me he really loved her and that I looked like her. He told me I was special to him just like his wife.

He also told me that my mom and dad would not believe me, and if I told them, they would not love me anymore. That lie alone kept me silent. All children want to be loved by their parents. I understood that they loved me but did not comprehend that they would ALWAYS love me no matter what.

I thought grown-ups always told the truth. I didn't want my mom to think I was a bad girl, so my lips were sealed, and my heart soon followed. This man not only taught me to lie to my parents, but also taught me that they could not be trusted. One lie leads to another and another. Even as a child, lies can cloud your mind in such a way that the truth is hard to find. It was those lies that had me bound.

I began to believe I was not lovable at all. The sense of shame that covers an abused child eventually covered me. The baby dolls and tea sets he bought me were probably to ensure my silence. Someday I would realize I was not special at all. I was a victim. I knew that something bad had happened to me, but I didn't understand what it was.

There were times when he was babysitting me that I got very upset. I would cry and beg for my mom to come home. That made him angry and when he when was angry, I was afraid. He always knew when my mom would be home, so he would stop hurting me and give me a chance to calm down. He wanted me to be smiling when she returned. He said he didn't mean to hurt me; he loved me. He told me that my mom wouldn't come home until I stopped crying. He would then seat me at the kitchen table with a crystal sugar bowl containing tiny little sugar cubes. I remember seeing sugar like this on my grandmother's table. When I was little, she would put those tiny cubes in her coffee. I stared at those perfect, little, white squares of beautiful crystals through the delicate prism of the dainty glass bowl from the dime store. They shined as I looked at them through my tears. I pretended to have a tea party. My long, blonde hair was pulled back into a ponytail and tears ran down my face as those little sugar crystals melted on my tongue. I could have as many of them as I wanted.

Sometimes he brought a loaf of cinnamon-raisin bread. In those days, we didn't have such a delight at my house. I would sit at the table and pick out all the raisins, put them into a little pile, and eat them. He didn't even care that I was making a mess. Eventually, I would stop crying and Mama's little girl was just fine by the time she returned. All that sugar made me feel better, at least temporarily. As I grew up, you can just imagine what I wanted anytime I felt bad.

We lived in Pennsylvania for eight years, and I guess about seven of those eight years were full of abuse. When we finally moved back to North Carolina, I was going into the sixth grade. This is a time of big change in most kids' lives. The sixth-graders were the oldest children in the elementary school, and all the other kids looked up to us. We thought we were "real big stuff." Sometimes the boys would laugh at the girls after they noticed they were beginning to look like women. I remember the boys being separated from the girls when we went to watch a movie about our changing bodies.

One day I heard a group of girls talking about another girl who was a couple of years older than us. One of them said, "She's a whore." They all laughed. I could tell by the look on their faces that it wasn't a good thing. I sure wasn't going to ask what it was, but I came home from school with that question on my mind.

Later that evening while I was waiting for my mom to finish cooking supper, my dad came home. He sat down in his big, overstuffed recliner to watch the evening news. This picture is so clear in my mind that it could have happened yesterday. "Dad," I asked, "what is a whore? I heard some girls talking at school today and they said another girl was a whore."

Sometimes my dad didn't respond to me at all when he was watching television, but that night was different. This time he heard me loud and clear. My dad turned around in that chair, and as his eyes met mine, I could tell he was very angry. I was not ready for the words that came next.

"They are women who allow men to use their bodies and they're just pigs." I felt the "P" in the word "pigs" as he spat it out. "That's very bad, and I don't want you to ever say that again." He didn't stop looking at me and I knew he wanted me to respond. "Okay, Daddy. I won't," I replied.

The words "use their bodies and they're just pigs" penetrated my heart as well as my mind. Instantly, I believed a lie that became the crux of my poor self-image. Even though I was only in the sixth grade, I thought I must be a whore. I wished I had never said that word. I knew something bad had happened to me, but I didn't know the word "sex" yet or what it was. I only knew my secret was something that made me feel ugly and ashamed. My dad had no idea what happened that day. He would have never wanted to hurt me. I walked away from him quickly to think about his answer. My dad would be so ashamed of me if he ever knew. Would he love me anymore?

I was determined that my dad must never know; my friends must never know. "It's all my fault," I thought, "I'm just bad." The girls at school were my new friends and they could never know my secret. This was one secret that had to be kept. I lived in fear. The isolation victims of sexual abuse experience is immensely traumatic.

My mind was spinning with mixed emotions. I really didn't know the truth from the lies that Uncle had told me over and over again. He said I was his girl and he loved me. Maybe he didn't know what he did was wrong or how bad he hurt me. How could he know? All this was going through my mind. The mind of a child! There was no way to understand and no one to help me. Uncle had successfully alienated me from my family as a young girl. He had controlled me.

One time my parents invited their old friend Uncle to visit us in North Carolina. I thank God that he never showed up.

The stories may be different, but the lies are the same. Some of you know exactly what I'm talking about. Those lies grow and grow. When you feel that you are unlovable, you separate yourself from the ones who do love you. Those lies came and those lies stayed. They became a part of how I saw myself and who I was. I had always been a gentle and obedient child.

Good girls obey, and good girls don't cry! I always did what I was told. I didn't tell anyone because I was told not to, but all of that didn't keep me from feeling like a "bad" girl.

There's a scripture that says, "For as he thinks in his heart, so is he" (Proverbs 23:7).

How could God change these thoughts?

I must be bad. I must be a "whore."

Chapter Three

THE PRINCESS IS LOST

You would think by this time there was a contract taken out for my soul! I will agree. There was a battle raging around me. The battle of good versus evil is timeless. There are some things that are very black and white in this world.

Ephesians 6:12 says, "For we do not wrestle against flesh and blood, but against principalities, against powers, against the rulers of the darkness of this age, against spiritual hosts of wickedness in the heavenly places."

Child abuse is one of those dark things. The future of a child (and therefore the future of a family and even generations) can be changed when the innocence of a child is stolen away. I heard a child predator say, "I never hurt her; she liked it." His perception was so warped he didn't see her (or his) innocence. He didn't even see that she was a child, and yet her whole life was changed forever.

When you are a child, people ask you, "What you want to be when you grow up?" As a little girl, all I remember wanting to be was a mommy and a missionary. How could all that goodness be so mixed up in my mind? There is almost no way a child can sort out all these feelings by themselves. Most adults are not able to sift through the mess and come up with the truth.

You have probably heard someone say, "Just get over it." They may mean well but they have absolutely no idea what they are saying. You also have probably heard someone say, "You'll never get over it."

I'm here to say that neither is true. With God's help, you can be healed. The journey may take a while, but you will get there. You will find your true identity.

With so much chaos surrounding my early years, did God really have a plan to pull me through? As I look back, I can see where He was working in my life.

Even in the middle of all this turmoil, I could still see a light. As a child, I can remember believing in God. I always knew God loved me. I can remember lighting a candle in a Bible study at seven years old and saying I wanted to shine for Jesus.

It was now time for junior high. I remember my best friend had been to a Christian camp for two summers. When she came home from camp the second time, she was filled with wonderful stories of campfires, cabins, boating, new friends, renewed friendships, and a stronger faith. I wanted to go with her the next year. Knowing the camp registration filled up fast, I asked for the next year's application only a few weeks after the season had ended.

The disappointment came when I saw how much the camp would cost. Then, I read the section that said there was a second option for applying. If your family really couldn't afford for you to go to camp, they had another way. All I had to do was receive a daily Bible study from the camp each week. I would have to read the study, answer the questions, memorize scripture, and mail it back at the end of each week. The study lasted for the entire school year. When summer came, you had a free trip to camp!

Wow, that was for me!

When I began, I had no way of knowing that by the end of the year, I would have memorized 300 scriptures. There was a checklist I used to make sure I knew them all. I would recite verses to my mom each night. I would put little pieces of paper in my school books so that I could read over my verses at school. What a wonderful plan God had to renew my mind and spirit. I just thought it was a free way to attend camp!

One of the first scriptures I learned was Jeremiah 29:11 which says, "For I know the thoughts that I think toward you, says the Lord, thoughts of peace and not of evil, to give you an expected end."

God had a good plan for me, and I knew I had not experienced it, yet.

The Word of God is Truth. That Word can heal your mind even if you don't understand how it could possibly work. There were so many lies implanted in me that it was like a hornet nest raging over my head. Have you ever seen a big, gray hornet nest? You can actually hear the hornets buzzing inside of the nest. There can be hundreds of hornets swarming around and around in there. On occasion, I've heard that they all come out at once. (My first reaction is that you better take off running!) If you can imagine, that's exactly what my mind was like. My thoughts went in every direction. Somewhere in that swarm of thought was the queen hornet, and her name was Abuse. I felt like I didn't fit anywhere. I felt torn and dirty. I knew sin raged in my heart and I wanted to be free of it.

One Sunday morning at the end of a church service, our minister gave an invitation to accept Jesus as our Lord and Savior. I knew I couldn't hold back anymore. On the third verse of the song, "Just as I am," I walked down the aisle and gave my heart to Jesus. Tears rolled down my twelve-year-old cheeks. I asked Jesus to change my life. I felt the presence of God like never before. I remember smiling until my cheeks hurt. I had a peace of mind that I had never felt before.

The following Sunday, my teacher asked me to share with my classmates what had happened to me. She asked, "Why did you go forward? Why did you walk down the aisle and go to the front of the church?" (This terminology may be totally foreign to you, but if you keep reading I'm sure you will understand.) I told them I knew in my heart that I wanted a relationship with God and that wasn't possible with sin in my life. I was sorry (repentant) and I told that to God. After I asked Jesus to come into my life, I felt like a new person. The heaviness of my sin was gone. I felt joy and peace in my heart. I had never trusted anyone, but now I trusted my life to Jesus. This was the BEGINNING of a journey that would last a lifetime. I was ready for a change in my life.

I never revealed my secret.

Over the next two weeks, twelve of my friends decided to accept Jesus into their hearts, and we were all baptized on a Sunday morning a few weeks later. That church was full of rejoicing parents. Maybe there was a little evangelist inside me. I do know that God has a plan for our lives.

I tried my best to forgive Uncle for what he had done to me. It seemed like it should have been an easy thing. I thought all those lies would simply disappear when I asked Jesus to come into my heart. I knew my sins were forgiven, but those awful thoughts still plagued my mind. The terrible memories were still there.

Although we may feel hopeless, God has a plan to completely heal us. That plan is not to just make us feel better for a little while. It took me years to find that plan. It was right there in His Word. It is so strong in me now that if you will grab hold of what I am teaching, you will be whole by the time you finish reading this book. I will help pull you out of the darkness of lies in which you live. The upcoming years will be spent enjoying what God has for your life. You will not be a victim anymore. You will become the one who helps those who are still hurting.

This may sound like just plain nonsense to you, but what do you have to lose? I have heard statements like, "But you have no idea what was done to me."

Oh! But I do.

The depravity of man stretches over a very wide band, but the love and power of God are without end. He knew that evil things would happen to us and that is why He made a clear way to get us out of this mess.

I think this journey of mine must have taken me all the way to the moon and back. Please allow me to lay out a map before you that will show you the way to wholeness and peace. There is no need for you to wander in pain and confusion.

Those teen years should have been wonderful, but with every year that I grew older, the mystery of what happened to me as a child began to fade away. That mystery was replaced with guilt and self-hatred. After a while, that hurt turned to anger and a confrontational young woman emerged.

Rebellion and anger poured out as I looked for someone to blame for all the hurt in my life. Our parents are usually our closest support as teens and they frequently bear the brunt of our anger. I really didn't have a clue why I was so angry, but I found ways to pour it out on a regular basis. I finally realized that Uncle really DID know what he was doing. He used me. He said, "You are special." I knew that wasn't true either, the abuse was for his pleasure. I had become so rebellious I really didn't want anyone telling me what to do. Deep inside, I blamed my parents, but I wasn't ready to reveal my secret. My anger overflowed toward them regularly.

There were images that were seared into my memory. They had stolen my peace of mind. Those images were of a beautiful, little blonde-haired girl, but they looked like child pornography! It was me! I would have done anything to make them go away!

All kinds of things would trigger the onset of a video in my mind. I remember as a teenager and young adult hitting my head with my fist. I can even recall a time when I hit my head on the wall. I guess the pain on the outside was not as great as the pain on the inside. I learned how to smile and pretend like everything was okay when I was only three or four years old! I learned to ignore my feelings and pretend. Sometimes it was hard to know what was real. I had become very good at deception and had a very hard time trusting anyone.

Every young girl thinks of being a princess. She was created to dwell in beauty and innocence. She was created to worship in the presence of God. When that innocence has been stolen, she loses her dream. When she looks in the mirror, she looks past her own beautiful face. She only sees the abuse. She sees something dirty and ugly. She's not a princess anymore. Maybe she never was a princess!

Many things can steal the innocence of a child and I do mean steal. The lack of a father in a young girl's life can send her to find love in all the wrong places. When families are torn apart in divorce, little girls are left behind. Some parents are so hurt themselves that they don't know how to show love. Pornography can steal that precious innocence away from a child in a minute. The pictures come back to haunt. No matter whatever or whoever the predator is, the lies are deposited into her soul.

Your soul is your mind, your will, and your emotions. When you feel unlovable, ugly, dirty, and angry, your mind becomes a playground for evil.

I've written about the war that I was in several times. I read my Bible, prayed, and yet I was angry inside. I lived in rebellion against my parents. I didn't even talk to my parents unless I had to. That doesn't sound much like my idea of a Christian. I understand now that I just didn't know how to give my hurt and pain to God the same way I gave Him my sin. I was torn by so much hatred, but most of it was aimed at me and I knew that I didn't want to feel that way.

I began this chapter by telling about the plans that saved my mind. Without those summer camp scriptures deposited into my heart, I would have had nothing to keep pulling me back to the truth. I thought the princess in me was gone forever, but God said that He loves me with an "everlasting love" (Jerimiah 31:3). If there was any hope at all, it would be found in Jesus. If there would ever be peace in my mind, it would be found in Him.

Where Are You, Lord?

Is it your fault, God, that I hurt so bad?
Where were you Lord as life went from happy to sad?
I tried to look for you, but I could not see, and all those hurts
    just blinded me.
I've cried buckets of tears until I could cry no more, then I dried
    my eyes and closed all the doors.
Inside I'll be safe, they won't ever hurt me again, the rest of my
    life, they'll never get in.
I shut out the hurt and shut out the pain,
but with it went joy and peace, and I didn't feel the same.
Lord where are you!? Are you still on the throne?
Oh, I'm waiting dear one. You have never been alone.
I cried as you cried, and I ached with your pain.
I wanted to comfort you, but you made me to blame.
I've given men a will that is free.
They can choose to follow or turn their backs on me.
As they choose the ways of this world and live in sin, all evil will
    come and enter in,
You were hurt my child by the sins of another, but I'm here
    today for you to discover,
Just how great a plan I have to redeem, and I'll heal you today
    and it will seem,
As though the things of the past which came to destroy, have
    become the strengths you now use, to bring others Joy.
All things will work together for good, and you've been called to
    do the things that only you could.
When you look at others, with My Eyes of Love,
You will choose to forgive, with my help from above,
Then for all of your hurt and all of your shame,
I will give joy, peace, and love and you will never be the same.
Come little lamb, Just as You Are,
I'm here right now; you've not gone too far.
-- L. G. Gibson

Chapter Four

A QUEST FOR WHOLENESS

I was the youngest student in my high school graduating class. I started the first grade at five years old in Pennsylvania. I could not have started in North Carolina that young. That made me only fourteen when I began the tenth grade. All of my high school friends were sixteen to eighteen years old. I talked to my parents into letting me date because all my friends were dating, and I soon found myself at parties with a much older crowd. Some of the twelfth graders had friends who were already out of school.

I accepted alcohol when it was offered to me when I was fourteen. I wasn't drinking because it tasted good; I wanted the feeling of being "high." My drinking was related to the abuse. (The bad choice was still my own.) All of the havoc it brought into my life and the ungodly things I did while intoxicated were my own responsibility. To me, getting high was a way to forget. But, as soon as you're sober the problems come right back, and in reality, they're usually worse.

A real turning point came for me at twenty-two years old. I realized I might not make it to thirty if I didn't do something to change my life. My body ached more like I was fifty instead of twenty-two. I had stomach ulcers, probably from drinking almost every day and stress. I knew that I wanted to be a good mother, but that couldn't happen the way I was living. I had been married at seventeen and had two children by then. I was soon to be divorced.

I cried out to God to please help me stop drinking. One day I went "cold turkey," as they say. I really didn't realize I had become dependent on alcohol, but after going three days without my beverage of choice, I was shaking and hurt something terrible! I couldn't even walk up a set of stairs to my apartment. My heart was racing. I was determined to make it through. I raised my voice and prayed over and over, hoping the God of my childhood would hear me again!

Not only did the desire for alcohol leave, but the smell of it made me sick to my stomach. I still hate the smell of any alcoholic beverage to this day. That desire was gone for good.

Without my heart healed from the past, you can only imagine that I fell back into the same relationship traps. I was desperate to feel love and security. I immediately entered into another relationship which was doomed to fail from the start. But, I had not forgotten what God had done for me and I didn't want to live without His guidance.

I began to study God's Word every day. When my children were napping, I read the Bible. Men had lied to me, but God would not lie. He is Holy. I must have forgiven Uncle a thousand times, but I was never sure it was enough. I had learned to control my anger, but it was still there. I thought maybe this is "as good as it gets" for a girl who was as emotionally damaged as I was. Someone once told me that since my dad had a temper, I probably took after him. They made it sound like it was one of those things you just couldn't control. I believed that God must have a better way.

I joined a small church and attended every service. One Sunday I was asked to fill in for a teacher who couldn't be there that week. I enjoyed reading, studying, and teaching that class. There was a gift of teaching in me, and it was immediately recognized. Throughout my twenties, I taught a class on Sunday mornings. The ladies were between eighteen and forty years old. I was moved to the forty- to sixty-year-old class before I was thirty years old. I'm sure I learned much more from those older ladies than they learned from me.

I came to realize that if I had a willing heart, God would use me at whatever stage of healing I was in at that time. I studied God's Word because I love to teach. Two more children were born during that time. I am so glad that none of them ever knew a mom who was a drunk, but they did know a mom who was still angry.

I would describe the anger in me like a pot that was barely simmering on the stove. Turn up the heat, and it could be boiling in no time. I had no idea why I responded the way I did, but I hated it. I knew it wasn't the way I should respond. I often exploded at my children. I became a screamer. After screaming at my children one time, I ran into my room and slammed the door. I lay across the bed and cried. Between sobs, I would ask God to take away the anger. My children hadn't provoked that response. It was just waiting like a volcano about to erupt.

I was sorry for the way I acted, but I just couldn't get it to go away. I remember crying in my room over my terrible behavior when two of my children got into a fight in the hall. By the time they were beating on my door accusing each other, I was boiling and ready to jump up and scream again, "Just leave me alone for a few minutes. I want to pray!" I knew there had to be a better way, but I just couldn't find it. It hurts to think I acted like that. This is bound to hit home with some of you. When you don't deal with what's really in your heart, it will grow into something that can hurt you and the ones around you. So, I learned to control that anger like a circus lion on a chain. I would grit my teeth and hold it in. I believed that was how to handle anger. You just learn how to control it. I never knew that if you were healed inside, you wouldn't have the anger issue anymore.

There were new issues to deal with on top of the emotional ones. How would I make a living for myself and my children? One thing that had somehow been set in my heart from childhood was a trust in God. That would not be easily uprooted, but it would be tested. When your bank account is in the negative, there isn't very much food in the house, every bill is due, and your kids need shoes, you find out in a hurry who you trust or if you trust anyone. That is where I found myself.

I love to paint, and at one time had an opportunity to paint watercolors and oil paintings for a local chapter of Ducks Unlimited. Several of my wildlife paintings sold, but it certainly would not sustain us. I had a showing in Richmond, Virginia and sold a few more of my paintings, but it was not enough to take "this show on the road." Now I knew what they meant by "starving artist." I not only loved painting, but I also loved to make crafts and decorate. I was really praying for God to show me what to do, and I believed I could somehow prosper from using the talents and gifts I had been given.

A friend of mine who had a booth at the Southern Living Christmas Show and the Southern Spring Show in Charlotte called me out of the blue and eventually hired me to create new Christmas designs for her business. This was right up my alley. I designed wreaths, baskets, window and door decorations, and other beautiful things to adorn the holiday table. I even worked her booth at the show and made personalized items to order as customers watched. The special orders really made the business boom. Most of my time was spent at home making things to refill the stock. That meant I was at home to see my children off to school and meet the bus in the afternoon. There was a deep desire to have a home business, but with little to no money it wasn't very likely to happen.

All the hustle and bustle of the holidays were over, and I realized my income from working for someone for a little over minimum wage was gone long before the month's bills were all paid.

My friend called once again, but this time with a different offer. She told me that she needed to help her husband with his business and was going to give up her booth before the next show. She was asking if I wanted to take her booth in both shows. This was a bigger deal than you can imagine because at that time there was a five-year wait to get into those shows. I said, "YES!" She even offered to pay for the booth up front for me!

I believed this was an answer to my prayers. With the spring show coming up in a month, I would have to work very hard to have enough inventory for the show. My parents quickly answered my call for help with this new endeavor. They were my bank. It took a lot of supplies to make what I needed with thousands of people coming to that show. I worked feverishly to get everything ready.

Country crafts were very popular during that time. I had a small woodworking shop, and I made wooden mama, papa, and baby bears with movable arms and legs. I painted faces and clothes on them. I made doll cradles, hand-painted wooden rocking horses, and hand-painted plaques with ruffles around them, as well as many other delightful goodies. My children had little jobs to help me, and we loved our little business.

Those retail prices were a welcome surprise at the end of the show. The last day of the show a very sweet lady approached my booth. I had seen her earlier that weekend as she walked past my booth looking at everything. I also knew she was a dealer by the badge that hung around her neck. She said she really loved my inventory and asked if I was represented on the wholesale market. I really didn't know what she was talking about, but I was ready to listen.

She told me that she represented several other people and took their products to the wholesale market with hers. She asked if I would like to make samples of my best sellers and send them with her to Chicago, Atlanta, Philadelphia, and back to Charlotte. She came home from the wholesale market with $10,000 in orders for me. I hired three ladies from my church, had UPS picking up at my house daily, and was shipping to twenty-five states. I REALLY WAS IN BUSINESS!

God made a way when there seemed to be no way (Phil.2:13, 14). Surely, if He would meet those financial needs for my little family, He would meet the need I had for wholeness.

If you are a victim of sexual abuse, you learn to cope in some ways in your everyday life. You try to lead something similar to a normal life. My friends did not know I was abused. My family did not know I was abused. They never could have imagined what had happened to me. For the first time, it seemed like I had my act together. After all, who knows what is fake with us or if our dreams are only fairy tales? I would have been satisfied if this good time never ended.

It may seem that you are still waiting for something good in your life. My heart goes out to the young women who are reading this. You're not alone. I thought I was the only one in the whole world who was in terrible pain and had secrets hidden inside. I soon realized the pain was widespread and I had a deep desire to help other women.

I began then, as a leader of a women's group in my own church. Later, I became the director of a young women's ministry involving twenty-five churches. I had the opportunity to be trained to work in a women's ministry in the North Carolina mountains at a beautiful retreat center. I also trained as a "Rape Crisis Companion." After over one hundred hours of training, I assisted doctors and police with victims when they were brought to the hospital.

As I grew in age and maturity, the images faded, and the anger was buried. I truly wanted to be used by God and be a good mother. Then one day my worst nightmare came to fruition.

Chapter Five

I GIVE UP

When my daughter was almost thirteen, she went to a conference for preteens and teens with her church group. Some of the time at this conference was spent in large groups, but there was also an opportunity to join "breakout sessions." One of these sessions was for girls only and she and her best friend eagerly attended. As you can imagine, they discussed things such as respect, inner beauty, and staying pure for the husbands they would someday have. They also brought up sexual abuse. The girls were told that if anything ever happened to them, they had to find someone in which to confide and were encouraged to go home and tell their mothers. This was one secret they should not keep to themselves. My daughter confided in her best friend while she was on the bus on the way home that night.

She had been repeatedly abused and was too afraid to let anyone know. I can only imagine those two young girls on that ride home. My daughter had the courage to do at twelve years old what I did not have the courage to do until I was thirty years old.

Her best friend went home fearful for my daughter's safety. She told her mother what had happened. I'm thankful that her mother was my best friend. She was a registered nurse at a nearby hospital and worked on the obstetrics floor with women. She called me that same night, and we talked for hours. Her daughter had told her the whole story. My daughter came home and went straight to bed. I don't think she wanted to face me right then, and I don't think I could have handled her emotions and mine that night. She finally had the weight off her shoulders and could sleep with peace.

That night I had to grab toward heaven and hold onto the grace of God. My mental anguish would not allow me to stay grounded. I knew my daughter needed me more than ever. The torment I was fighting for her was more than she could have ever known. My pain did nothing to cease hers.

Every lie I had ever heard regarding my motherhood, my worth, and my goodness was thrown at me all at once.

How could this have happened?

I tried to be a good mother!

I tried to always have my eyes and ears open to danger!

It must be my fault!

Evil follows me!

And now it has attacked my baby!

Oh God, where are you?

Nothing seemed to comfort me. Only condemning words pounded in my head. I can't think of anything short of death that was worse than to have my child abused. I wanted to be able to help her, but all I could do was search for that place deep inside me where I went to as a child.

A place where I could hide...

I wanted to pretend I was asleep and couldn't feel anything. I needed to be a big girl and dry those tears, but I had just become that little girl who had never been healed. I curled up into a ball and finally went to sleep near daybreak.

The next day my daughter would not let me cuddle her or comfort her. You see, she was just like me. She was in pain and she was angry. I was the one on whom she focused her anger.

Sin had come full circle. I didn't know I was still so wounded. I tried to find a place of comfort in the Lord, but I just couldn't get there. Several months had passed and it was now the day after Christmas. That afternoon my daughter lashed out in anger at me. I knew she was in pain. It was my fault. She even said, "It is all your fault."

She blamed me for what happened to her. This time I had no problem agreeing with her. She was just a child and had no idea what I had gone through myself. She was crying out for help. I could barely help myself much less anyone else.

In each chapter, I have made references to the confusion that was in my mind.

Are You Experiencing That Same Confusion Right Now?

My thoughts were swirling like the tiny tornadoes you see in the yard when dust and leaves cover the ground. All of the sudden, the wind begins to swirl and lifts the dust and leaves into the air. They swirl around and around, lifting higher and higher, until suddenly, the dust and leaves just go off in every direction. Thoughts can be like that in an unstable mind. If you are there, your thoughts are caught up like those little tornados, and you have very little control.

I felt like I was to blame for it all. I was just a bad mom. She would be better off without me. When such a trauma has been pushed down for years, IT DOESN'T JUST GO AWAY! It grows like a cancer. No one could know the agony I was suffering. I felt useless, hopeless, and helpless! Suicidal thoughts flooded my mind. I believed my parents could take better care of my children than I could.

That day after Christmas, the tree was still in the living room. I left my beautiful daughter and three wonderful sons sitting in front of the television watching a movie. I told them to go to bed when it was over. I went to bed early and locked myself in my room. I had been crying for hours and could hardly see through my swollen eyes. I took everything out of the medicine cabinet. There were over-the-counter sleeping aids and prescription drugs. There were some painkillers from past surgeries and even an antidepressant I tried at one time. I took them all and fell asleep crying. Right before I fell asleep, I called a friend whom I had promised weeks earlier that if I ever felt like I just couldn't make it anymore, I would call her. She was not at home and I left a message saying, "I'm keeping my promise, so I called you. Goodbye."

My hurt and pain would finally be over. Hopelessness convinced me that they would all be better without me.

I drifted off to sleep. An hour or two later, I could hear shouting and pounding on my bedroom door. It was like a faraway dream and I couldn't respond at first.

"Mama, answer the phone. The phone is for you. Please answer the phone!" I felt like I couldn't move, but I did manage to pick up the receiver. My children hung up the other phone. I kept trying to understand what was being said to me. It was my friend checking in to see if I was all right. The children said I had gone to bed earlier, and they just thought I was half-asleep. I couldn't understand a word she said. The longer I tried to stay awake, the more nauseated I became. I finally hung up the phone, staggered to my bathroom, and began to vomit up some pills. (None of them were digested yet.) I staggered back to my bed and fell into a deep sleep. I didn't wake up until sixteen hours later.

Praise God I woke up!

I felt horrible as I was waking up. What have I done? I knew I had tried my best to commit murder. I was not my own! I belonged to Jesus. I sobbed and sobbed and repented and repented. I knew at that point I needed help. I called my best friend who had talked me through that first terrible night when my daughter poured her heart out months earlier. Her prayers and support for me kept me going. I still wasn't in a very good state of mind, but I would never let those controlling, hopeless thoughts rule over me ever again. I could have been robbed that night of a wonderfully rewarding life forever.

A few days later, Heaven touched earth in that very same bedroom.

Chapter Six

HEAVEN TOUCHES EARTH

The new year had just begun, and I had done a tremendous amount of soul-searching. I wanted to be whole if there was any way to be whole. I needed my damaged emotions healed.

If I Couldn't Find Peace In My Own Life, Then How Could My Beautiful Daughter Ever Find Peace In Hers?

I knew that God's Word was true. God's Word says, "God is not a man, that he should lie..." (Numbers 23:19). I had to find a way to grab hold of it for myself. I had ministered to abused women. As a trained Rape Crisis Companion, I worked the twenty-four-hour hotline. I told them what God had in store for them. I wanted to help those young girls who had become prostitutes on the street. I couldn't tell them they could have "the peace of God, which surpasses all understanding..." (Philippians 4:7), when I had little to no peace myself. I believed by faith that they would have it, but now I needed to experience it for myself. If I still saw the terrible images in my mind, then why shouldn't they see them in their minds? If those ladies were able to walk away from prostitution, they shouldn't be doomed to see their "Johns" in their minds for the rest of their lives! Would they someday lie in bed with their husbands, but still see the faces of other men? What kind of victory would that be?

Would my daughter see horrible degrading images also?

I needed answers!

Surely, God had a plan!

The One who created the earth knew my heart. The One who set the stars in place knew what I needed.

One night after my little angels had been tucked into bed, I went to my room to talk to God. I got down on my bedroom floor and began to pray. I began to pour my heart out. Those memories that I internalized for years and years began to overwhelm me.

Have you ever been surprised by the force of soda that sprays out of a bottle once it has been shaken? I was overcome by a fountain of emotion as I began to talk to God, just as though I were one of those bottles spewing.

I found myself describing what had happened to me as a child. I told God what I went through as if He didn't know or had not been there. I had not allowed myself to go to those dark places and repeat what I saw there. It looked like child pornography.

Tears rolled down my face as I spoke the UNSPEAKABLE. Those images made it almost impossible to talk. Sometimes it seemed too bad to even let the words form, so I just thought of it knowing God knew my thoughts. It was like a cancer inside of me had been eating me alive. As I wept on the outside, something else was going on the inside. I became angrier as I spoke. Finally, I looked up and shouted out, "Where were you?! Where were you?!" My voice was lifted toward Him as tears ran down my cheeks. "Where were you, Lord? Why didn't you just strike that man dead? I loved you! I prayed every night as a little girl!"

My voice quieted to a whisper as I sobbed in a heap on the floor. I was overwhelmed with a sense of abandonment. Only a tiny whisper could be heard as I repeated, "Where were you? Where were you?" All the anger was just rolling off my tongue. I had no idea I was mad at God. I loved Him, yet I was blaming Him for all that hurt. I guess I always had. Then, to my surprise, I began to hear God speak to me. His voice was so clear that I wondered aloud, "If anyone were here, would they hear Him too?" His presence filled the room.

"It Was Not Your Sin. You Were Not To Blame. I Gave Man A Free Will. I Did Not Create Him To Be A Puppet. I Spoke Into That Man's Ear And Said, 'Stop! Stop! Don't Do This To Her.' He Chose To Ignore Me. I Cried As You Cried. I Hurt As You Hurt. It Was Not Your Sins But The Sins Of Another. Right Now, Tonight, I Will Heal You If You Let Me. Forgive Him For What He Did To You."

I cried out, "I forgive him, Lord, I forgive him! Lord, please forgive me for blaming you. Please forgive me. I know it was not your fault." My eyes were swollen with tears and my face was buried in the carpet, but I could see as clear as day. I began to see a movie playing in my mind. Some would say I saw a vision.

The Vision:

God was sifting sand through His fingers. It was like the sand on the beach you make castles with as a child. Water began flowing over the sand like it was being poured in a small stream from a glass. He began to mix, moving His hands back and forth on the ground as if to mix mortar. Then, He picked up a big block and put the mud on it. It was all in the palm of His hand. He mixed and placed until He had laid one block on top of another and another.

"I'm Making A Platform To Stand You On, To Minister Healing To Others. Right Now I Am Going To Heal Your Memories If You Allow Me To."

It looked like the block pillars in the foundation of a house. Then, I saw Him pick me up in His hand like a little china doll and set me on top of that foundation. He used my past to make my future! It was beautiful! A peace flooded over my soul. It rose up from deep within me and I began to worship my Creator. Before I even thought of what I was saying, I realized I was thanking Him.

"Thank you, Lord, that you are healing me from that abuse, for it is through that healing you're going to heal others. Thank you, Lord! Thank you!"

It may sound unbelievable, but in that moment, it did not matter what had happened to me. Because I was so covered in God's love and grace, that abuse did not exist. There is no abuse in Heaven and at that moment it felt as though Heaven was in my bedroom.

Ever since that night, my mind has been free from the tormenting images of my childhood. The glory of my healing is that although I know what happened, it is so distant that it is like it never happened to me at all. It was someone else. There's no pain, sorrow, or shame associated with it.

The anger left me that night. I was no longer begging God to take it away! That anger was gone. It had been all tied up in my unforgiveness and my misdirected anger toward God. I believed a lie that told me, "It was all God's fault. He doesn't love you. He didn't protect you." I believed He didn't really love me or even care about me. Now I knew just how much He loved me and just how much He loves us all.

All my pain was wrapped up in lies and I finally had the key. The devil is a liar and the father of all lies (John 8:44). The truth will set you free (John 8:32).

Only God can use the things that were meant to destroy us to bring wholeness to others (Romans 8:28). I am whole, and God is using me to bring wholeness to others.

Chapter Seven

GOD'S PLAN FOR US

Truth had been a long time coming. I wanted complete wholeness in my mind and my emotions. In that one night, God exposed lies in me that had been there almost my entire life. He told me that this was not my fault.

I believed I must be evil because bad things kept happening to me.

I believed I was a bad girl.

I believed somehow, I could have stopped my abuser.

I believed that God didn't care.

I believed my parents didn't love me.

I believed the future was lost.

I believed my mind was scarred forever.

I believed I was a bad mother.

I believed I was just damaged goods.

I believed shame would be a part of me forever.

I could go on and on!

All of those lies were what God used to mix the mortar and lay the block on which He placed me. Those lies fell like dominoes as I stood with them beneath my feet. God restored my innocence. There is no psychiatry or drug that can heal minds or delete memories. Only God can lead us through the canyons of our minds.

Many of us once had paper maps or an atlas in our car. Now nearly everyone has a GPS either in their car or on their mobile phone. We make sure we always know where we are going. We trust the GPS to lead us in the dark. God is our GPS in this life. He really did leave us detailed instructions for what He has for us. Why not follow them before we fail? I know I want to follow His lead.

Our Map to Healing

In Isaiah 61 and in Luke 4, we are told just what Jesus came to do for us. These two scriptures were written about 800 years apart. These may be the most important scriptures you will ever read. Please don't skip a word. Read them and read them again.

Isaiah 61:1- 3: "The Spirit of the Lord GOD is upon Me, because the LORD has anointed Me to preach good tidings to the poor; He has sent Me to heal the brokenhearted, to proclaim liberty to the captives, and the opening of the prison to those who are bound; to proclaim the acceptable year of the LORD, and the day of vengeance of our God; to comfort all who mourn, to console those who mourn in Zion, to give them beauty for ashes, the oil of joy for mourning, the garment of praise for the spirit of heaviness; that they may be called trees of righteousness, the planting of the LORD, that He may be glorified."

Luke 4:18-19: "The Spirit of the LORD is upon Me, because He has anointed Me to preach the gospel to the poor; He has sent Me to heal the brokenhearted, to proclaim liberty to the captives and recovery of sight to the blind, to set at liberty those who are oppressed; to proclaim the acceptable year of the LORD."

In the above scripture, "recovery of the sight to the blind" is describing physical healing. (I'll touch on that later.) All the other things mentioned in these verses have to do with our minds and emotions. I was brokenhearted, mourning, and being held captive in my mind. I was bruised. I was able to accept salvation, but I had never known how to accept the other gifts God had for me.

After reading aloud the passage you just read from Luke, He (Jesus) sat down and closed the book. He continues in verse 21, "And He began to say to them, 'this Scripture is fulfilled in your hearing.'"

The plan God has for us doesn't just include one thing or even two things. It includes everything we need to be whole. God wants to restore our lives in every way. It is for God's glory that He will do these things for you and for me. Hear what I am saying, it's for His glory!

Christ came in the flesh to the earth to fulfill these words. He first came to preach the gospel message. I call it, "The Plan of Salvation." It is for all who would receive it. That's what I received as a little girl. I believe, because of sin, we all need a savior.

Romans 3:23 says, "For all have sinned and fall short of the glory of God." We are born into a sinful world. We don't have to teach our children to disobey, lie, or steal. We must teach them not to. We naturally rebel against our parents. It is part of the nature of sin ever since Adam and Eve in the Garden of Eden. It should be a freeing to understand that God was a perfect parent, the Creator, and they still disobeyed him. No matter what rules are set, children will disobey at some point. God knew we would continue to sin, so he made a way out for us. He sent His only Son.

John 3:16 says, "For God so loved the world that He gave His only begotten Son, that whoever believes in Him should not perish but have everlasting life."

Verse 17 says, "For God did not send His Son into the world to condemn the world, but that the world through Him might be saved."

Most of the churches in the world preach this message. It was after hearing it that I gave my heart to God. He cleansed me of my sins. If you've never experienced this love, you can do it right now. Jesus gave His life so that we can come before a Holy God. He loves us that much.

If you would like to invite Him into your life today, you can pray, "Lord Jesus, I believe you are the Son of God who came to take away my sin. I repent of my sin, all the bad things that are in my life. I ask you to forgive me and take away my sin. I want to live my life for you. Please come into my heart right now and show me how to live for you. I love you, Lord. Amen."

The Bible says there is joy in heaven when even one person accepts God's gift of salvation (Luke 15:7). From this moment on, your life can and will be different. Seek His will for your life. He has so much more for you. The verses in Isaiah and Luke tell us many more things that Jesus has for us. I gave Him my sin. He gave me eternal life, with Him.

We Are Three-Part Beings

God created us as three-part beings. Our spirit will live forever. Our soul is our intellect, our will, and our emotions. Our physical body is the part that tells me quite often that I am getting older. Spirit, soul, and body. God always had a plan to restore us completely, all three parts. The question is, will we allow Him to do just that?

One thing that keeps us from allowing God to heal us is rejection. As a child, I thought my family would reject me if they knew the truth about me, so I distanced myself from them emotionally. Somewhere deep inside, I also thought God had rejected me. When we feel rejected, we tend to reject the people around us. Relationships can be quickly sabotaged. We walk away from family and friends before they walk away from us. We say things like:

"They don't want me in their life."

"They don't really care."

"They don't like me."

"I am not important to anyone."

Rejection is a spirit that works to separate you from the ones who love you and keep you from forming new relationships. Rejection causes pain.

Do you recognize any areas of your life where rejection has destroyed friendships? Have you felt like there has been a wall between you and those you love? It is time for the walls to come down!

Chapter Eight

HEALING BROKEN HEARTS

It is almost impossible for us to make it through childhood without receiving a broken heart somewhere along the way. A little girl says goodbye to her daddy one morning, not realizing that his suitcases are in the trunk of his car, and he will never come home again. A first-grade boy with beautiful red hair is picked on, unmercifully, by his classmates. Another is picked last every time a team is chosen. In fact, they usually argue over who has to take him. A mom is dying of cancer, and her little girl isn't allowed to see her one last time. She just wants to say "goodbye," but no one understands.

Children receive broken hearts every day. If somehow you made it through childhood without being scarred, there is another battleground when you become an adult. Do you look back on certain events in your life and tears fill your eyes or anger wells up inside you?

Is the pain still there?

Does it feel like it just happened yesterday?

You were wounded. Your heart was broken. We've heard the old saying, "sticks and stones may break my bones, but words will never hurt me." Broken bones will heal, but words can last a lifetime. Those words shaped your future. God's Word says, "Death and life are in the power of the tongue..." (Proverbs 18:21).

There are only two places in the whole Bible that the word "brokenhearted" is used. They were both quoted in Chapter Seven and are powerful scriptures. Isaiah 61 and Luke 4 say that Jesus came to heal the brokenhearted. God does not want us to go through life broken. It clouds up everything in our life. It affects how we see things and how we respond to those around us.

As a little girl, I thought my parents didn't really love me. My abuser told me that if I told my parents, they wouldn't believe me, and they wouldn't love me anymore. In my mind, that made me unlovable. I most certainly knew the secret, even if they didn't. So, I never felt loved! My heart was broken! My mom later told me that I would rarely talk to them as a child. They didn't know why I was so unhappy. I cried a lot. My family thought I was just very tender-hearted, but I was brokenhearted. There is a big difference.

Think of it like this...

You could have the strongest bucket ever made, but if it has a hole in it, all the water will drain out. When someone has a broken heart, you could tell them a hundred times a day that you love them, but when they wake up the next day, they will still feel unloved. If they were abandoned, you could be the most faithful person in the world, but they will still believe you will leave them. Their broken hearts must be healed.

When I studied the Hebrew and Greek text in which Isaiah 61 and Luke 4 were originally written, I found out that "brokenhearted" means to be crushed completely or shattered into little slivers.

Several times, I have broken a bowl in my kitchen that shattered into slivers. The only thing that could be done was to sweep up the slivers and toss them into the trash. No matter how well I tried to clean, there were always little slivers left behind that found their way into my foot. It's a real mess to clean up. I've also had other bowls that have been accidentally knocked off the counter and broken. They only broke into a few big pieces. One such bowl is on my counter. I glued it back together. Although it has a few ugly cracks in it, when I turn it around to hide those flaws and fill it with fruit, you cannot see where I had glued it back together. It can never be used for its original intent as the centerpiece for my table. I keep it tucked away on the counter where you can only see one side.

I also have a flower vase that only holds silk flowers because it will never again be able to hold water. Although the broken pieces were glued together, water still seeps through the cracks. Without water in the vase, I can't feed fresh cut flowers from my garden. It will never again be used for live flowers or to its fullest potential.

You could say that these are "damaged goods."

God didn't make some fancy super glue to put our lives back together. He had a perfect plan that makes us brand new. We don't have to be glued back together and then hope to be used for something or anything at all!

His plan is perfect!

It Is A Gift!

At my house, I just love Christmas. I'm excited to see a present under the tree with my name on it. Sometimes, I pick them up and give them a little shake, hoping to figure out what's inside. That gift may be mine, but it is totally useless to me unless I take it out from under the tree, unwrap it, and claim it as my own. That beautiful blue sweater will never keep me warm until I put it on. Then it is truly mine.

We have to receive the precious gift that God has given to us, that it is truly ours.

When you're ready, close your eyes and pray,

"God, you know how I feel. Please show me where this broken heart came from."

Begin to describe to Him what you're feeling. Talk to Him and know He is listening to you and He will answer you. Remember, He was there.

You might feel afraid, sad, or even angry. Allow yourself to experience one last time the flood of emotions that are attached to that brokenness. There's a lie attached to what happened to you. Ask God to help you think of that lie that you have believed. You will know what it is. You have heard that lie over and over. Sometimes it may seem like the truth because it's been there so long. The little girl whose daddy left her waving goodbye believed she did something wrong to make her daddy go away. That was a lie.

There is a TRUTH for every lie you have ever heard.

The young boy, who was never picked by anyone on the team, grew into a man who believed he was just a loser. That man became a pastor. Most of the time, he wasn't quite sure if the people in his own church wanted him. He had been fighting a spirit of rejection his whole life. Even when he did his best and felt God's presence when he ministered, the minute he finished, the enemy came quickly to tell him that the people didn't like what he had to say. People were blessed by him, but it was hard for him to believe. The pastor prayed and asked God to speak truth to him. He heard God speak to him and say, "You are my first choice. I pick you." In his mind, he could see himself as that little boy, and Jesus coming right onto that ballfield and pointing directly to him. God had picked him to be first on His team. God showed him that the spirit of rejection had planted the seeds in his life to keep him from being the mighty man he was created to be. He let the lies go and grabbed a hold of the TRUTH as the Lord showed it to him. He is now bringing healing to many wounded hearts.

Sometimes we know exactly when and where that broken heart came from, but other times we just don't remember. Once a woman told me, "I just feel ugly. I have always believed that no one would ever love me." She could not remember why she felt this way. God showed her in prayer one day where that belief came from. He showed her why she believed such a lie.

The lies we believe can go on and on, but God will speak truth to us if we will listen. He will speak truth to you right now. John 8:32 says, "And you shall know the truth, and the truth shall make you free."

When the truth comes, lies must go. We then have to forgive the source of the wound. It may be those kids who mocked you in school or the dad who left or was abusive. All of us need to be forgiven.

Mark 11:25-26 speaks to us about God's forgiveness.

Verse 25 says, "And whenever you stand praying, if you have anything against anyone, forgive him, that your Father in heaven may also forgive you your trespasses."

Verse 26 says, "But if you do not forgive, neither will your Father in heaven forgive your trespasses."

When God spoke to me He said, "It was not your sins but the sins of another." I knew then that I did not have to accept responsibility for the sins that I had not committed. I had believed I was a bad person because something bad had been done to me. That was a LIE! I had to ask forgiveness for my own sins and forgive the ones who have sinned against me.

Allow God to show you the difference.

Many times, I have led women (and men) through the process of forgiving the people who had hurt them. I comforted them as they cried. We walked through steps of forgiveness and found healing for their minds and hearts. God will meet you right where you are when you call out to Him.

I ministered to a lady who had been with a professional counselor for eighteen years because she had been abused by a family member. She had been a Christian for many years. She was a wonderful teacher. Even after many years of trying to receive healing, she was not able to receive it. In a few short hours of walking through the Word of God together and praying, she was able to receive the gift of truth and healing that God had for her.

It was like that beautiful Christmas present I described earlier that always had her name on it, but she had not been able to open it. As she opened it and the truth flowed over her, she was healed deep down in her soul.

Receiving the healing God has for you will change you in every way. This lady not only received healing for herself, but as a teacher and a principal of a school, was able to bring healing to many. In every area of her busy life, God was able to bring hurting people along her path.

Remember the beautiful bowl I had broken that was never able to be put to use for what it was intended? Until her healing, she never had a use for those ugly super glue marks on her back. Now you can turn her in every direction and only see beauty! God can now use her to the fullest extent of what He had created her to be, as she in return offers counsel to others in need.

That is exactly what God does.

John 8:32 says, "And you shall know the truth, and the truth shall make you free."

Truth comes.

Lies go.

You are made whole!

Chapter Nine

MERRY-GO-ROUND OR POTTERS WHEEL

Many times, you have probably heard someone say, "I'm sick and tired of being on this merry-go-round." You may have said it yourself.

There is a shopping mall in the area where I once lived. In the middle of that mall was a food court, and in the center of that food court, was a beautiful carousel. The bright-colored horses were decorated beautifully, and multi-colored lights flashed as the children went around and around. As the music played and the lights flashed, every child within hearing distance tried to get to that merry-go-round. I'm sure it was designed that way. Between the smell of french fries and the sound of the music, it was almost impossible to get a child out of there. I have ridden beside my child on that merry-go-round many, many times. As a mom and a grandmother, my job was to stand beside them and make them feel safe as that horse went up and down and around and around.

There was usually someone who wasn't on the carousel who was nice enough to wave at us every time we went around. The merry-go-round would start out slow, but as it turned, it would speed up. There was no way to get off until the horses were finished with their run. Around and around and up and down they rode. By the fifth or sixth time around, I was ready to be done with it, but the children never wanted to get off. They loved every minute of it.

It's okay to take a ride on the carousel and maybe even take a second turn, but at some point, you're going to have to get off. When you grow up, it seems just useless to go around in a circle, over and over again.

I heard a woman say, "I just keep choosing the wrong man." Another said, "People continually walk all over me." And another, "I can't tell you how many times I've been victimized." They seemed to settle for much less than they could have in this life.

I remember one lady who was abused as a small child, raped as a teenager, and married to an abuser. That's what I would call "calamity upon calamity." What was going on here? Was there no end to it? She was on a merry-go-round. Sexual abuse seemed to follow her. It really did. One time I heard her say, "Do I have a sign on my back?" She had become a victim over and over again, and now her children were victims.

Going around and around in circles may make a little child happy, but it makes most adults feel like failures. Are you sick and tired of the ride yet? Let's stop this merry-go-round and get off!

When you realize the pattern of your life is a pattern of destruction, it's time to step forward and believe for a change.

Let God help you make a change. Doing the same thing over and over and expecting a different outcome is defined as insanity. God knows the truth as to why you can't move forward in your life. Allow Him to speak into your life again. Replace the lies you hear with the truth. You may need to ask His forgiveness for not trusting Him with your life up to this point, but know that in His hands you'll be safe.

The Bible says that God is the Potter and we are the clay. Isaiah 64:8 says, "But now, O LORD, You are our Father; we are the clay, and You our potter; and all we are the work of Your hand."

Jeremiah 18:2-6 shows us that God is like a potter who can even shape a nation on the potter's wheel. Surely, if He can shape a nation, He could shape me!

Allow yourself to be shaped on the potter's wheel. You have already been changed on the merry-go-round, and it usually isn't for the good. You are full of disappointments and hopelessness from repeating the same mistakes over and over again. Trust your Creator, the One who can mold and shape your life. Become pliable in His hands. Yield to Him as He touches every area of your life. He will form you into a vessel of honor.

Just like pottery, I'm sure, He had to lay me down on that wheel as it turned. He would sprinkle some water on me to make me pliable, and then He turned and turned the wheel. I felt His gentle pressure as He molded me this way and that way. Sometimes, it felt as though He touched me deep inside as He rooted out the darkness hidden in the chambers of my heart.

Can you visualize yourself on His wheel, going around?

Close your eyes and observe His hands holding you and molding you. The water He pours over you is likened to the flow of His Spirit. He's rubbing off all your imperfections. He is making you smoother and smoother in every area of your life. Clay becomes pliable when water is poured over it. The Holy Spirit is like that water. He will flow over you as God molds your life into something new.

You may be at a place in your life where this sounds a little scary. To have someone's hands upon you may make you fearful, but God, your Maker, can be trusted. He loves you with an everlasting love. You are safe in His hands. As the days go by and you recognize that there are things in your life that keep popping up, you can rely on Him to mold you and change you.

God wants to heal you completely.

Pray:

"Lord, it's time for me to get off this merry-go-round. Please lift me from this wooden horse to the Potter's wheel. I am willing to allow You to mold me into the person You created me to be."

There are times when we did not get on that merry-go-round alone. We may have been on that ride with our parents or grandparents. In some cases, they may have even been the ones who put you on that ride. We may have watched that same horse circling endlessly in their lives as well. If you look back through the generations of your family, you may find that abuse, abandonment, or alcoholism, etc. shows up over and over. These are things that have been passed down for generations.

Ephesians 6:12 says, "For we do not wrestle against flesh and blood, but against principalities, against powers, against the rulers of the darkness of this age, against spiritual hosts of wickedness in the heavenly places."

You are a child of God; you have the right to break those things off your family - forever!

Pray:

"Lord Jesus, in Your Name, I ask that You remove the (abuse, incest, alcoholism, etc.) from my family, never to return. I confess the sins of my forefathers and I want to break them off our lives. I want to live for You, Lord, and I don't want this darkness, this SIN, passed down to another generation. I don't want my children to experience these things. I want a better life for them, Lord, and for all future generations. In the Name of Jesus, I ask for all these things to be broken off my family forever. Amen."

I want to tell you a story about one of my children when he was small. It's a perfect example of how we know what's right, yet we keep going back and doing what's wrong.

My son was fourteen months old, and we were still trying to teach him "No!" regarding our television and its remote control. He was like all the other toddlers that had come along. He really wanted to push those buttons.

One of my older sons was very tender-hearted. His pattern had been to retreat in tears at a stern look and a little "grunt" noise. Another sibling would have touched it over and over, believing that I would get tired before he would. He was like a little bulldog, proving many times to be a strong-willed child.

On this particular day, the fourteen-month-old was circling the living room jabbering on and on. He was wearing only a diaper and running quickly in and out of the room. He looked like a shark closing in on its prey. He made all kinds of sweet baby noises with so much expression that I knew he was in deep concentration. He would circle around, darting toward the television. He stopped just in front of the television with his arm outstretched and his little fingers pointing toward the buttons on the object of his fascination, wiggling it around. His jabbering never stopped. He got so close, I just knew his fingers were going to touch the forbidden device, but instead, he slapped his own tiny finger with his other hand, yelling to himself, "No!" He had his head down, shaking it towards the floor as if to say, "No! No!" again and again.

He had stopped himself from touching that button! Wow!

He never touched it at all.

He ran off talking to himself. After a few minutes, I heard him coming back down the hall. He was still talking to himself and this time he wasn't circling the room. He ran straight toward the television, pushing the forbidden button! He then ran and hid behind the big recliner. I couldn't help but laugh. I held my hand over my mouth. I didn't want him to hear me. He was in a real struggle. He hid himself behind that recliner and didn't look like he was coming out any time soon. He just kept jabbering and jabbering, perhaps fussing at himself about what he had done wrong.

Isn't this much like us? We run around and around the very things that we know that are going to cause us trouble. We focus on that one thing that's going to bring harm to us or pull us back into our old lifestyle of sin.

I sat on the couch thinking about what had just happened with my little one. He continued to sit on the floor behind the recliner, sounding as if he was giving himself a good talking-to. I knew I had to confront him about what had just happened.

First, I had to stop laughing!

I pulled him out from his hiding place and set him on my lap. I explained to him again why he could not touch the television. I didn't want him living in disobedience or hiding in shame!

Some of you are still behind that recliner in your parents' living room. The shame you live with from a bad decision you have made is keeping you there. You don't have to walk in sin and shame. Accept responsibility for what you have done wrong and receive God's forgiveness. Then, forgive yourself and the ones who have wronged you. Remove yourself from the room where the television is located (or your specific temptation). There are so many other rooms in the house or opportunities to occupy your time. Don't obsess over those temptations! Don't hide in shame. Find a friend you trust, a person who will pull you out from behind the chair if you ever go there again. Please don't stay there! We don't have to live in shame.

Come out, come out, wherever you are! The game is over! You are free!

Chapter Ten

NO LONGER HELD CAPTIVE

Fear can hold us captive in such a way that it gives life to the lies that we have embraced. Being a prisoner in our minds can lead us to being paralyzed in some other areas. The longer the fear feeds on those lies, the more they have control over us. There are all kinds of lies that control our lives. Sometimes we don't even realize that the lies have ensnared us.

As a young woman, I remember being very spontaneous. I could pack a bag and head for the beach in another state on very short notice. That never bothered me. I didn't have to make plans very far in advance and I never kept a calendar. It was a wonder I kept any appointments at all. As the years went by and my children grew older, there were too many activities going on for me to be so unorganized. I began to maintain a calendar, trying to keep everything in order. I then realized just how much keeping appointments cramped my style and restricted my liberty. I would break my appointments often and reschedule for a day that I thought was better. Sometimes I had no legitimate reason to change them; I just didn't want to do it right then. The thought never crossed my mind that I had a problem until appointments were scheduled that just couldn't be changed. It made me feel very anxious. At that time in my life, I had already learned a lot about lies and truth and how they affected me. I usually listened for the truth and easily found it in most situations. I never dealt with this discomfort (keeping a set agenda) until I felt like I was going to have a panic attack upon realizing I had to keep my dentist appointment.

"That's it!" I thought, "I have a problem!"

I remember thinking that maybe God was trying to show me something. Maybe one of the kids is going to need me, I reasoned. Maybe something bad would happen while I was on the road. My list of reasons went on and on. I couldn't really pinpoint anything because I was in a state of confusion.

I knew that fear does not come from God and at the root of my feelings was fear. Believe me, I was not feeling of "sound mind." I did, however, keep my appointment with the dentist that day and nothing terrible happened to me.

Soon, I even began to become fearful if my husband had to go somewhere. I had no idea what was going on, but I knew I had to get to the bottom of it. Something was feeding the anxiety and it grew bigger and bigger. I finally realized I was being controlled by fear in this area of my life. I found some time alone and began to pray.

I closed my eyes praying, "Lord, there is something in my past that's causing me to avoid scheduling. I keep changing these appointments. Please show me what it is. I don't know what's wrong with me."

I began to see a picture in my mind of a little girl whom I quickly recognized was me. I was about four or five years old and I had long blonde hair. I was standing on the steps of the home of the man who molested me. My back was to the house, facing my mother. I was looking up into my mother's beautiful face. She bent down over me and put one hand on each cheek, tilting my head towards her face. She looked into my eyes and said, "Be a good girl! I have an appointment. I will be back to get you after a little while. Take your nap and do what you're told. I'll be back to get you as soon as naptime is over."

As I saw that little girl standing there and heard my mother's words spoken to her, I began to cry and tremble. It was as if I was right there standing on the steps. My mother had absolutely no idea that when naptime came, I had to get in that big bed.

Something awful was going to happen to me. She would not come back until it was over. When I was there, I had to pretend to be asleep so that, just maybe, he would go away, and it would all be over quicker. When I saw myself on those steps, I felt helpless. I couldn't move, and I couldn't even pray. I was four years old and helpless! I felt like there was a lion only a few feet away in that doorway. I could not help myself. I was only a child.

I decided to call a good friend and prayer partner. I was still very disturbed as I told her what I had experienced. I told her that I was stuck on those steps in fear. She began to pray with me. She asked the Lord to show me where He was and for Him to speak truth to me.

My cry went up as tears rolled down. "Oh, Jesus, where are you? Please, show me where you were while I was waiting on the steps so frightened and alone."

Immediately, in my mind, I could see Him right behind me. He picked me up in His arms and whispered in my ear, "You never have to go there again. It is all over now. He can never hurt you again." Then, while He held me, we turned around and the whole place was gone. I opened my eyes. All the fear had vanished! I didn't feel helpless anymore!

The Lie:

The lie I had believed was that something bad would happen to me because of an APPOINTMENT. That word was attached to my fears. It was a big word for a four-year-old child.

The Truth:

The truth was the man was bad. The sinful thing he was doing was bad. It was that simple!

My mom had no idea what was happening. I forgave that man one more time. I also forgave my mother for putting me in danger, even though she did not know she was doing so.

All that darkness had been exposed. I never remembered the words that had been spoken to me before that day. I could have gone for years with hidden fears that were ruling my life. This is how phobias take over people's lives. Doctors and pills do not expose the LIES that control us. When they are left hidden, they grow like a cancer. Some people are so controlled by them that they cannot even function.

When I heard the truth, the lie disappeared. All my negative feelings regarding appointments were immediately gone. I was truly held captive in that area of my life. The lies that held me captive were the lies that I had believed.

When my friend prayed for me, she also commanded any tormenting, lying spirits connected to that event to leave me. I immediately felt totally at peace. I have been free from those fears since that day. The lies that hold you may be different, but the outcome is the same. You may find that you have been paralyzed in some areas of your life.

A Little Boy's Story

A mother brought her son to me one day to help discover what lies he had been believing. When they were getting ready to move halfway across the United States to North Carolina, a friend gave this little six-year-old boy a beautiful picture book about the new state where he was moving. He looked at pictures of the beautiful mountains, and he saw the rolling waves of the ocean. He saw beautiful flowers, streams, and creeks. He was amazed at all the birds and spiders, and even snakes. By the time he moved into his new home, he had studied that book many times.

Instead of being excited to be in his new home, he was unhappy and didn't even want to go outside and play. He refused to explore his new backyard. He didn't want to go to a nearby park. His mother said he was so fearful, that he would run to catch the school bus in the mornings and run back to the house in the afternoon.

Over a year had passed, but he never wanted to go outside and play. It was like he was a prisoner in his own home. Before he moved, he would play outside for hours. His mom had no idea what was wrong. His whole personality had changed. He hadn't made any new friends.

I met him and his mother at church. She even had a hard time getting him out of the house to go to church.

She said it was almost as if he was going to have a panic attack upon leaving the house. He began to cry and scream and begged to be left alone. I told her I'd love to talk with him if she didn't mind. So, I sat down with this precious child. I told him that Jesus wanted to take away his fears and that He was going to show him a little video in his mind. I asked him if he was willing to watch and see what Jesus would say. He said, "Yes."

I prayed, "Lord Jesus, will you show him where this terrible fear came from? Please show him why he doesn't want to go outside anymore and why he is so afraid."

I told him to keep his eyes closed and watch the pictures that Jesus would bring to his mind. He began to curl up in the chair in which he was sitting. He pulled his knees all the way to his chest and wrapped his little arms around them. I asked him, "What's going on in your video?"

He told me he saw a picture of himself at the beach with his family. I asked him how old he was and what was going on. He said he was about three years old and it was just about dark and there were little crabs running all over the beach. They ran and crawled into little holes as the waves crashed up onto the sand. Everyone was laughing except him. He was so afraid of the crabs.

He became anxious and said, "I couldn't get to my mom because she was way across the sand and the crabs were between us." His voice was cracking as he tried not to cry. As I looked on, big tears rolled down his cheeks and he trembled in his chair.

He pulled himself into a ball and fell over into the fetal position. I prayed again, "Lord Jesus, will You show him where You were? He needs to see You right now." Immediately, the little boy began to smile. He still had his eyes closed. Then, he even giggled a little bit. A few seconds later, the grip around his legs loosened and one of his legs dangled off the chair. He sat up.

"What's happening?" I asked.

"Jesus picked me up in His arms and carried me to my momma," he said. "I didn't have to be afraid. Jesus said, 'I'll take care of you. The crabs never bit you, as I was there, and I will always be here for you.'"

The little boy opened his eyes and his whole countenance was different. He began to tell me about his book about North Carolina. He saw spiders and copperhead snakes, and he even saw an alligator. He thought all those things were lurking just outside. Now he wasn't afraid anymore. He realized that Jesus had always been there.

Jesus sets the captives free! Even a seven-year-old boy!

The next time I saw him, he was smiling. He told me that he had begun to play ball with the children at school. Now he didn't act afraid of anything.

Jesus spoke truth to him, and the darkness of fear left.

In his mind, the snakes and spiders in the book were crawling all over the place, just like the crabs that ran on the beach. He told his mom that he wasn't afraid anymore because he knew Jesus was watching over him and protected him. His mom was thankful she had her little boy back.

Your circumstances will be different, but the bars of fear that hold and paralyze you are just the same. You won't be able to do what God created you to do while you are held captive. Jesus has the keys. Let Him set you free today.

Chapter Eleven

OPEN PRISON DOORS

Isaiah 61:1 says, "The Spirit of the Lord GOD is upon Me, because the LORD has anointed Me to preach good tidings to the poor; He has sent Me to heal the brokenhearted, to proclaim liberty to the captives, and the opening of the prison to those who are bound;"

To those of us who have been abused, lies are the very bars that keep us imprisoned. I personally have been locked in a room while being abused, but I was eventually released. The lies that keep us prisoners can last a lifetime. They follow us everywhere and affect everything we do.

Ask the Lord to reveal to you any such lies. "Is there anything still here Lord?" Now, stop and listen.

The Lord will speak to your heart. He will show you if there's anything still there. Are you ready to put those lies behind you and live the life God has given you without being held back?

There is an easy way to check yourself to see if you are really healed. Just think of one of the things that used to bring you to tears, one of the things that God has already shown you the truth about. If you are free, you will not feel any emotions about what once overwhelmed you. As those thoughts enter your mind, it may even seem like it happened to someone else.

As an adult, I hated to sleep in a room with a mirror on the wall. I didn't want to see my reflection. I wanted the lights left off. My abuser had mirrors, lots of mirrors on every wall of the bedroom. One wall was solid mirror tile. I saw a frightened little girl trying desperately to cover herself when I looked in the mirror. As a child, I closed my eyes tightly, so I could not see my reflection, wishing I could not feel anything either. A mirror was like a portrait of child pornography, and it was me.

I was not able to do something as simple as look in the mirror at my own reflection. Wouldn't you say that I was being held prisoner?

When God healed that little girl in me, she was no longer stuck behind the looking glass. I no longer see her, no matter how hard I try. God instructed me to gaze into that mirror and I saw myself through His eyes. I saw the woman who He created me to be. I was no longer held prisoner by those pictures but free to do His will.

There are so many lies that can hold us captive. I am very thankful that God can free us from them all.

Let's explore the image we have of ourselves. What lies do we believe? For example, "Do I look sleazy?" I hated to try on new clothes. I wanted to look pretty, but every time I looked at myself I just felt like I looked "sleazy."

When I went shopping, I could have tried on clothes all day. I put one thing on and took it off, put another on and took it off. For some reason, nothing seemed to look right to me. I remember at one point in my life, for about two years, l wore long fluffy skirts and big shirts. I looked sort of like a pilgrim! Guess what? Even when I looked like that, I still felt sleazy.

One day my husband was shopping with me, and I came out of the dressing room wearing a beautiful new dress. I said to him, "Do I look sleazy? Do I look like a hooker?"

That particular day my husband said, "What's up with the sleazy?"

"I just don't want to look bad. I don't want to look like a hooker. I don't want to look sleazy!"

"You couldn't look sleazy if you tried," said my husband. "It's a matter of the heart, and that's not your heart. It's okay to look like the beautiful woman you are. There's nothing about you that is sleazy. You are beautiful."

I began to weep right there in the store. The Lord took me back to that day in my parents' living room when that eleven-year-old girl heard her dad give the definition of a whore, "They are women who allow men to use their bodies and they're just pigs."

Those words had penetrated my very soul. That was a lot for a sixth grader to understand. That was the very year we moved back to North Carolina. That was the year that my abuse finally stopped. The enemy told me a lie that day. He told me I was a whore, and I believed it.

My parents might have been able to help, but the abuser's lies created a gap between us that was just too wide for my adolescent mind to bridge. I stood in the department store as that scene flashed before my eyes. Right then, I remembered it was not my sin. God had told me it was the sins of another. I realized it was a lie that I had believed to that day. The truth was that I have never been sleazy, and I was never a whore. The shame that came with how I felt about myself had to be healed.

TRUTH is like an ax that God lays to the root of our negative beliefs and the lies that fashioned them.

I was a woman washed in the blood of Jesus (I John 1:7). I was now as white as snow and I would help change the lives of others through my own experience.

Prisoner Set Free!

The lies that hold you captive are not the same as mine, but they will hold you back just the same. The enemy uses the same tactics over and over again because they work. Women, for thousands of years, have felt worthless because of abuse. It was never God's plan for His creation to feel worthless, whether they be men or women. It is Satan's plan!

Our Creator knows our value, so let's listen to Him and what He has to say about us. I don't want to listen to what the enemy says anymore. Christ came to open prison doors. He came to set the captives free. He only speaks truth to us and that truth sets us free.

He set me free!

"Was I Born This Way?"

This question has been asked of me over and over again.

I felt like I was bad because bad things kept happening to me. Conclusion: I must have been born bad.

We are born with original sin, but we're not born to be bad. These feelings can be deceiving. Original sin came from Adam and Eve.

Romans 3:23 says, "For all have sinned and fall short of the glory of God,"

Romans 5:8 says, "But God demonstrates His own love toward us, in that while we were still sinners, Christ died for us."

We were created in the image of God with a purpose. We all have need of a Savior.

Something evil happened to me as a child. That does not mean that there was something wrong with me. The pedophile wanted a child to fulfill his selfish desires, and I was the convenient one. I was the one least likely to cause him trouble. That does not mean I was born to be a whore, or born to be a prostitute, or born to be a victim!

I recently talked to a man who was molested at a young age by an uncle. He began to do what had been done to him to his cousin. He was convinced that he was born a homosexual because his uncle had sought him out to abuse him. "I must be homosexual," he thought.

He was not born to be a homosexual any more than I was born to be a whore because someone had molested me. This is the same type of spiritual lie that made me believe that I must be a whore. There were unclean, perverse spirits that attacked our lives because of what happened.

Those lies are from the enemy. Lies hold us captive to keep us from becoming who God created us to be. They become part of our thinking when the abuse happens. I keep emphasizing "LIE." If you do not get to the root of the problem, you will never be set free.

Someone had used this young boy for his selfish desires. That made him a victim, not a homosexual. Sexual abuse invites a spirit of sexual perversion into our lives. That spirit then takes up residence, and the lies keep it rooted in the very fabric of our heart, psyche, and belief system. Sexual perversion is a very strong spirit and along with it follows pornography, child pornography, adultery, fornication, addiction, and all sorts of other evil activities.

God Has A Better Way!

God created our sexual desires. He created our sexual pleasure for the marriage bed and in that marriage bed; there is no guilt or shame. It is the place where we connect with each other through bonds of love. A beautiful relationship within these boundaries is much like a worshipful experience.

Please don't be robbed of the wonderful gift that God has given to a marriage. It is sin that turns sex into a dirty and shameful thing. I have known young men who after being molested became the most sexually active people you will ever know. Each night they would try to lure another girl into their web of seduction. This would go on for years and years. When they finally admitted they had a problem, they also admitted that it started when they were abused. The words, "You are homosexual because of the abuse," went through their minds over and over again. They believed that because someone had used them, they might be homosexual. So, to prove to themselves that they were "straight," they continually had sex with women. They were not looking for love but only to vindicate themselves. Sexual perversion and lust are strong drives. Perversion can take you in any direction you're willing to go.

I had a practicing homosexual tell me that he could spot another gay person in a room full of people. He called it "gaydar." That declaration was absolutely of no surprise to me. After all, couldn't a man also spot a promiscuous woman from the other side of the room?

Spirits can find "like" spirits. A homosexual spirit could identify a like homosexual spirit as well as a spirit of perversion and promiscuous sex. The enemy has a plan behind this evil and a network to bring it to pass. When you follow after perversion, the outcome will always be the same: YOU WILL FIND IT! Eventually, the lies that you've heard in your mind will become truth to you. GOD HAS A BETTER WAY! The Bible says, "For as he thinks in his heart, so is he" (Proverbs 23:7).

When someone enters into a lifestyle of perversion, it may seem like he or she can never escape, but God has a way out. Fear and the enemy's lies give power over their circumstances.

Faith In God Gives Us The Power To Hear The Truth And To Act On It!

When we ask God to forgive our sin, He does. His Word says that He remembers it "no more." Our sin is as far as the East is from the West (Psalms 103:12). It is buried in the deepest sea (Micah 7:19). God does not have a memory problem! He chooses to remember our sin no more!

Confess the sin, let the lies be revealed, and hear God's truth and embrace it. The enemy has no choice but to leave. Those spirits only dwell in the darkness. The lies and the sin are the darkness for them to reside. When their dwelling-place is gone they cannot stay. The light of Jesus comes in where the darkness once was.

In the name of JESUS, they must go!

The captives are being set free every day. I am so glad that I was one of them.

Today is your day!

I love the scripture in Jeremiah 1:5. It says, "Before I formed you in the womb I knew you; before you were born I sanctified you; I ordained you a prophet to the nations."

Imagine, God knew you and formed you. He loves you even when you are in sin. It is not too late to watch Him transform your life. He has a plan for your life and it is a good plan.

Jeremiah 29:11 says, "For I know the thoughts that I think toward you, says the LORD, thoughts of peace and not of evil, to give you a future and a hope."

The prison doors that have held you bound like the ones in Isaiah 61 will be open even as you read. When you seek after the wholeness that is through Him, He will make you brand new.

Isaiah 61 also says that it is His will to make us whole as it is to show the world, so that "He might be glorified." Our shattered lives don't bring much glory to God. I know my shattered life didn't, but a life that's been made whole has brought glory to God.

Let's get the real picture of the exchange that's going on here.

I give Him lies and He gives me truth.

I give Him brokenness and He gives me wholeness.

I give Him sadness and despair and He brings me joy.

2 Corinthians 5:17 says, "Therefore, if anyone is in Christ, he is a new creation; old things have passed away; behold, all things have become new."

Chapter Twelve

THE GREAT EXCHANGE

God's plan to restore our lives was designed even before we were ever born. His plan was not to patch us up like an old tire, knowing that it could still blow out at any time. His plan is to make us brand new. There is a great exchange that was made for us. 2 Corinthians 5:21 describes that Exchange:

"For He made Him who knew no sin to be sin for us, that we might become the righteousness of God in Him." This does not speak of a superficial exchange. What is said here takes us down to the very core of our being. First, we are changed spiritually then our soul man can follow.

Isaiah 61:3 says, "...to give them beauty for ashes, the oil of joy for mourning, the garment of praise for the spirit of heaviness..."

The Great Exchanges to fulfill His plan:

- Joy for Mourning

- Beauty for Ashes

- Praise for Heaviness

Joy for Mourning

Webster's Dictionary definition of *mourning: an expression of grief; as if mourning the dead.*

That pretty much describes how I felt about my life when it had been shattered by abuse. After the abuse, you mourn for yourself. You mourn your failed relationships. You mourn for the life that wouldn't have been so difficult if only "it" had not happened. You mourn for that beautiful, little child and her innocence. You mourn for the adult who is still in pain.

The word "mourning" may make you think of people dressed in black cloaks and grieving for a loved one they lost. For me, it was as if that happy little girl died within me. We are told in this verse that mourning, ashes, and heaviness can be replaced by JOY, BEAUTY, and PRAISE. I received that myself and now it's your turn!

Beauty for Ashes

A victim leaves a trail of sorrow and darkness everywhere he or she goes.

Ashes are left behind after a fire in my old wood stove. When I try to clean the ashes, a black mess is left behind on my floor, my hands, and sometimes on the top of everything in the room. This black mess reminds me of the trail of sorrow and darkness we as victims tend to leave behind.

Webster's Dictionary definition of *beauty: a quality, attributed to whatever pleases or satisfies the senses or mind.*

After your abuse, has it been hard to identify the qualities of beauty within yourself? These were the very things that were stolen from you. It's time to find hope and be restored. Are you prepared for things that were stolen from you to be returned? This exchange is permanent!

It is not pretend or "maybe!"

This is a true exchange!

God says, if you will give Him the ruins, then He will give you a new life!

When I talk about a true exchange, it reminds me of going to a money exchange while I was a missionary in India. We were instructed to always go to a valid money exchange or a bank to exchange our dollars into rupees. There were always people around who were offering to exchange our money. They claimed that they would give us a higher percentage or a higher rate of exchange. Young men with big smiles would be waiting near the bank. They were hoping to get our attention before we went inside.

They had hands full of money and a very persuasive message, "Let me help you, I give you a great deal!"

We watched someone passing dollars to him. He counted the rupees quickly back to him and then swiftly went on his way. The gentlemen smiled for a minute until he looked down and began to count his money. He was sure he had made some extra cash, but when he finished counting his money, he realized he had been cheated significantly by the exchange agent's sleight of hand. He looked in every direction, but the thief had vanished.

How many times have you run after a better deal only to find sorrow when it was all over?

The valid money exchange was the only way we could ensure that we weren't taken advantage of in India. In your own life, you have to give God your ruins for a valid exchange of beauty!

This is a true exchange!

Praise for Heaviness

The word "heaviness" in Isaiah 61 means an obscure darkness. The heaviness comes with the sadness, the sin, and the lies of the past.

Webster's Dictionary definition of *praise: to command the worth of, or express approval or admiration... to glorify: to extol.*

Remember, this is an exchange. I had to give my dollars for the rupees. You have to let go of the lies to hear the truth. You may see yourself as a victim. It may have become your identity, but it is not the TRUTH of who you were created to be, or who you really are.

As I received my exchange, the heaviness lifted from me. I literally felt as if a warm blanket of praise and thankfulness surrounded me. My very soul was thankful to the One who had healed me. God wrapped me in a blanket of His love. I became so thankful for the freedom God had given me. I was finally free to worship and to love.

I urge you to do so right now. The lies are being expelled as you hear the truth, and that truth will set you free.

Right now, you can pray, "God, please lift the heaviness off of me. I feel like I am carrying a heavy weight on my back. I want to be set free and I want to be an instrument of praise. God, please take all the ashes out of my life and replace them with beauty."

Remember John 8:32 says, "And you shall know the truth, and the truth shall make you free."

You can trust him! He will not let you down.

It's okay to look or glance at your past, but when you GAZE on the Lord, fix your eyes on Him and you will be able to see clearly.

Trade your mourning for joy.

Trade your ashes for beauty.

Put on the Garment of Praise for the spirit of heaviness.

Receive what has already been made available to you.

The last part of Isaiah 61:3 reads, "...that He may be glorified."

Remember, God wants to restore you so that the whole world will know that He is your Healer. He is your Creator, Almighty God. He loves you with an everlasting love!

Through your healing, everyone will know how much He loves you. They will see His plan for your life. God only gives good and perfect gifts!

That Garment of Praise is put on so that we can say:

"It is God who did all these things for me."

"It is God who healed me."

"It is God who restored me."

"It is God who showed me a better way to live."

"It was so that He might be glorified."

Remember, this is an exchange. "Put on the Garment of Praise" means for us to begin to have thankful hearts. It is hard for us to be thankful when the things that have happened around us or to us are bad, but if we begin to speak out with gratitude and praise to God for even small things in our lives, we will recognize more and more good things. Start very simple if you need to. An example would be to say, "Thank You, God, for loving me." There is absolutely nothing that man has to offer that could heal my mind or yours. God and God alone can make this exchange.

Chapter Thirteen

SIGHT TO THE BLIND

Luke 4:18 says, "The Spirit of the LORD is upon Me, because He has anointed Me to preach the gospel to the poor; He has sent Me to heal the brokenhearted, to proclaim liberty to the captives and recovery of sight to the blind, to set at liberty those who are oppressed."

There are many ways that we can be blind, but I believe that in this scripture Jesus is speaking of the physical healing of our sight. There are numerous books that have been written about physical healing. Many go into great depth teaching the scriptures regarding this subject.

They spur your faith to help you know that it is available from God. I will not attempt to write another book on the subject in this chapter. What I will do is explain the possible connection to your abuse.

I'm sure you have heard that our emotions can be connected to physical sickness in our bodies. I believe many times they are. I had such an experience. My physical abuse was directly connected to a physical illness.

For twenty plus years, I had chronic cystitis (what most of us consider a bladder infection or UTI). Many of you know how painful that can be. I was always on the verge of getting an infection, suffering from an infection, or getting over an infection. Most often, I used a natural cure of vitamins and herbs, or changed my diet instead of using pharmaceuticals. It seemed that no matter what I used, it worked for a while, and then just failed.

I had been to the doctor many times and as a last resort, I allowed the doctor to put me on a low dose of antibiotics. It was just one pill a day, but I would probably be taking it for the rest of my life. I know what antibiotics do to your immune system which is why I had only taken them as a last resort. I couldn't keep the infection under control. By now, my body was weak from fighting the infection over and over again. It was one of those cases where I was sick and tired of being sick and tired.

I am sure you have been there.

After a few days of taking this low dose, I had a breakthrough, but it wasn't because the infection was gone. I was lying in bed talking to my husband. I had commented on how I really needed God to heal my bladder infection. If He would just show me what was going on in my body, I could get rid of it. I asked my husband to pray with me about it.

I immediately saw a picture in my mind. It was me as a little girl. I was in my abuser's home, and I was sitting on top of his big bed. I saw a picture of something that had happened to me. It was something that I was never willing to acknowledge. It was actually too disgusting to even speak about. It was even too embarrassing to repeat out loud to God. Now God had brought it into my mind.

"I see that, Lord! And I choose to forgive him for that! Yes, even that!"

Tears rolled down my face and right then, I knew this was the key to my physical illness and my physical healing. My husband continued to pray for me. When he prayed for me this time, it was a different prayer. That night I knew I would be healed. God showed me that this was how my body had reacted to the abuse. The Light had been shone on the darkness. When that darkness left, my healing came. I never took the antibiotic again, and I did not have chronic cystitis again!

I heard the testimony of a woman who was very emotionally damaged as a child. She was diagnosed with multiple sclerosis as an adult. Later, when her emotions were healed, so was her body! Our bodies are amazing because they were created by an amazing God! We are three-part beings and each part is connected.

I. Our Spirit-man

II. Our Soul

   a. Our Mind

   b. Our Will

   c. Our Emotions

III. Our Physical Body

If we accept Christ into our lives, our spirit-man has been promised eternal life with Him. When our minds and emotions are healed, we will be delivered from addictions and other tormenting problems that have come our way. When we trust Him and believe, we can be healed physically as well. Bitterness and unforgiveness will not only eat away at our emotions in the soulish realm, they can also cause physical illness. Did you know that many cases of mental illness are the result of bitterness and unforgiveness? Our trauma does not have to be what shapes our lives into who we become. It does not have to define who we are!

Romans 8:28 says, "And we know that all things work together for good to those who love God, to those who are the called according to His purpose."

ALL THINGS! This is a very powerful statement. You might say, "How could my abuse work toward any kind of good in my life?" This book is an example of ALL THINGS working together for good in my life, even though I was abused. When we seek to be totally free, God will walk us through all the dark places and bring us into the light.

When physical healing is what you are seeking, ask God to show you what you need to be whole. Jesus took our sickness upon Him on the cross so that we may be healed. He already suffered for our healing. I am so thankful that God made a way for us to be totally whole.

Here is a list of scriptures regarding healing. Read them and believe!

Exodus 15:26: "and said, 'If you diligently heed the voice of the LORD your God and do what is right in His sight, give ear to His commandments and keep all His statutes, I will put none of the diseases on you which I have brought on the Egyptians. For I am the LORD who heals you.'"

1 Peter 2:24: "who Himself bore our sins in His own body on the tree, that we, having died to sins, might live for righteousness—by whose stripes you were healed."

Psalms 118:17: "I shall not die, but live, and declare the works of the LORD."

Praise Him for His excellent greatness!

Proverbs 16:24: "Pleasant words are like a honeycomb, sweetness to the soul and health to the bones."

Thank Him for what He has already done for you!

Philippians 4:6: "Be anxious for nothing, but in everything by prayer and supplication, with thanksgiving, let your requests be made known to God;"

Praise Him for what He has done for you!

Psalms 113:1-4: "Praise the LORD! Praise, O servants of the LORD, praise the name of the LORD! Blessed be the name of the LORD from this time forth and forevermore! From the rising of the sun to its going down the LORD's name is to be praised. The LORD is high above all nations, His glory above the heavens."

Receive what He has already done for you.

Chapter Fourteen

HIS COVENANT TOWARDS US

I could not finish without explaining one of the most amazing things that God Himself has done for us.

Webster's Dictionary definition of *Covenant: a binding and solemn agreement, made between two or more individuals. And the promise made by God to man, as recorded in the Bible, to promise by Covenant.*

John 3:16 says, "For God so loved the world that He gave His only begotten Son, that whoever believes in Him should not perish but have everlasting life."

This covenant was initiated by God, not man. God first made this covenant with Abraham. He promised him a seed (a child) and land. God promised to protect and provide for Abraham and his descendants. A covenant is stronger than a promise or a contract. God cannot break His Covenant!

Covenants are talked about in the Old and New Testament. The Bible tells of a beautiful friendship between Jonathan and David.

Samuel 18:3 says, "Then Jonathan and David made a covenant, because he loved him as his own soul."

When men made covenants with each other back then, they didn't just sign a piece of paper like men sign a contract today. They would exchange robes, swords, belts, and armor. Each item exchanged had a meaning. They were saying to each other, "I will fight for you, cover you, and protect you from your enemies. I will be there to strengthen you." They would cut their hand or wrist to say, "I am your blood brother. I will die for you or your family." A bull was then sacrificed, and they would hold their swords towards heaven and shout, "God, do to us what we have done to this bull if we break this covenant." That promise was not only for David and Jonathan, but for their families, as long as they were alive.

After King Saul and his son Jonathan were killed in battle, David hunted for Jonathan's son for years, so he could make good the covenant he made with the father. Normally, in those days the former king's family would have been executed when the new king came to power. Jonathan's son's nanny was unaware of the covenant and expected David to come after the child to kill him. She was ignorant of their bond, so like a good nanny, she ran to hide the child. In the midst of their escape, she tripped and fell on him, crippling him. Ignorance of the covenant caused this child to be crippled for life. Ignorance of the covenant ultimately caused him to be a beggar living in fear of not being able to sustain life.

Jonathan's son was grown when King David finally found him. David had him brought to the palace to be fed at his table for the rest of his life. This beggar went from the street to the Palace. I did not say that Jonathan's son came for dinner or even a visit. His son would live in the palace just like the king's own family. David hunted him, but it was to love him and restore him to a place of honor.

Has Our Ignorance of God's Covenant Caused Us to Run from Him In Fear?

It's time for your restoration! If a man can keep a covenant with another man, then our covenant with our Creator is unbreakable!

We are given a new identity. Our identity is in Christ. We are called Christians and His Bride.

Read this beautiful scripture about the covenant.

Isaiah 61:10: "I will greatly rejoice in the LORD, my soul shall be joyful in my God; For He has clothed me with the garments of salvation, He has covered me with the robe of righteousness, as a bridegroom decks himself with ornaments, and as a bride adorns herself with her jewels."

Earlier in this book I talked about what I call, "The Great Exchange."

We give God our sin and He gives us eternal life.

My righteousness is like filthy rags, but He clothes me in His Righteousness.

Most of the time I have nothing to give but He loves me unconditionally!

He will give me beauty for ashes.

My mourning will be exchanged for joy.

I belong to Him forever!

He protects me from my enemies.

He will supply all my needs.

I can trust Him completely.

He will help me when I am tempted.

I am a new person. I have put off the "old man" and put on a new man, according to the One who created me (Colossians 3: 9-10). This is a Holy Covenant. It was designed by God to restore sinful man unto Himself. God knew He would not be able to allow sinful men to enter heaven. Sin was forever cast out of Heaven with Satan and the angels that followed him.

Our way to Heaven was made through the shed blood of Jesus Christ on the cross at Calvary. God, in the form of man, made a new covenant with us.

He Initiated This Covenant Toward Us and It Cannot Be Broken!

It is up to you to accept it!

Jesus said in John 10:27-30, "My sheep hear My voice, and I know them, and they follow Me. And I give them eternal life, and they shall never perish; neither shall anyone snatch them out of My hand. My Father, who has given them to Me, is greater than all; and no one is able to snatch them out of My Father's hand. I and My Father are one."

When we understand what God has for us, we will realize it is much more than a promise. This covenant will not be broken.

Have you entered into the Covenant with Him? Would you like to?

Let's get started!

Chapter Fifteen

LET'S SUM IT UP!

In this chapter, I want to outline the plan I have given you for wholeness. I will be reiterating many of the things we learned in the proceeding chapters about emotional healing. This may seem too easy, but God says we can come to Him with the faith of a little child.

Matthew 18: 3-4 says, "Assuredly, I say to you, unless you are converted and become as little children, you will by no means enter the kingdom of heaven. Therefore whoever humbles himself as this little child is the greatest in the kingdom of heaven."

It will not take any more faith to have your mind and broken heart healed than it did for you to ask Jesus into your life and believe in Him.

Success Strategy: Please read this chapter and then go back and follow step by step to your restoration.

If reading my testimony has been emotionally hard on you and brought back feelings that you have hidden for years, then please ask a loved one to read it also. Allowing them to be with you as you walk through these prayers will provide you much-needed support. It is very hurtful at times to look into those dark places within our lives and admit how bad things really were. Just don't forget, Jesus will be there with you every step of the way. I believe this will be the very last time you will have to look into those dark rooms in your minds. Jesus will turn the lights on!

In John 8:44, Jesus says the enemy is a liar and the source of all lies. In John 10:10, He says that the enemy is a thief. Through the Great Exchange, that thief and liar is going to be exposed within your life. Jesus came to give your life more abundance.

Success Strategy: Please have a pad and pen available before you start. You will want to create two columns. In the left column, write down the lies as the Lord shows them to you. In the right column, write the truths.

God's Truth cancels out those lies.

I am also providing a little writing space for this here:

_____

_____

_____

_____

_____

_____

You have probably already thought of many lies that you have believed in the past while you were reading. I hope you've already asked Jesus to show you the truth to replace some of those lies. But if not, I'm going to walk you through that process right now.

Begin with this prayer:

"Lord Jesus, I invite You to be in control of this time of healing prayer. I want to spend it with You. Please lead me. I want to hear Your voice and Your voice alone. The enemy has spoken lies to me, and Your Word says that the truth will set me free. Please speak truth into my life because I want to be free. In Jesus' name, Amen."

Continue Praying:

"Lord Jesus, please show me each lie that I have believed about myself. Take me back to the place where I began to believe."

Be Still, Listen, and Wait.

Let the video play in your mind. Some lies are exposed when we see what happened in our minds. Play the video of memories in your mind.

Now, one last time, hear that lie and then write it down. You may have to remind yourself that it is just a lie. When you hear it, say, "Yes, Lord I hear it. Now, please speak truth to me," or "Yes, Lord I see it."

_____

_____

_____

_____

_____

_____

Example of a LIE: "It was my fault because I was bad."

TRUTH: "It wasn't my fault at all."

_____

_____

_____

_____

_____

_____

_____

Now take time to forgive each person as God brings them to your mind. Luke 6:37 says, "Judge not, and you shall not be judged. Condemn not, and you shall not be condemned. Forgive, and you will be forgiven."

_____

_____

_____

_____

_____

_____

_____

This is an extremely important step.

Many times, I have heard, "They don't deserve to be forgiven," or "They aren't even sorry for what they've done!"

And you are right, but we don't deserve what God has done for us either.

I've heard unforgiveness described as someone taking poison and expecting the other person to die from it. That describes unforgiveness very well. The unforgiveness eats away at us, and the other person may not be suffering at all.

You want to pray, "Lord, as an act of my own will, I choose to forgive_____" Put their name in the blank.

This took me a very long time as there was a parade of faces that came before me and I needed to forgive each and every one of them. I was even one of them! There was a lot for which I needed to forgive myself.

_____

_____

_____

_____

_____

_____

_____

_____

Ask God to forgive you for your sins and the decisions you made while you were living in sin.

Ask God to remove the images and the bad memories from your mind. Be very specific. There are some images you never want to see again, and you should never have to.

Ask Him to heal the damage that was done by the enemy.

You will want to identify some of this damage as emotional damage that includes mental illness and your on-going fear.

Ask for healing and deliverance from all addictions.

Now it's time to break the cycle of sin within your family lineage that has been passed down from generation to generation.

In Exodus 20:5-6 it says, "...visiting the iniquity of the fathers upon the children to the third and fourth generations of those who hate Me, but showing mercy to thousands, to those who love Me and keep My commandments."

What is now happening in your life can change the lives of countless others.

When we're healed, our family members can now be healed. Generations can be restored!

Pray:

"God, I confess that the abuse, immorality, alcoholism, abandonment, drug addiction, are all sin. I ask for forgiveness for these sins, and I ask for every curse and every evil spirit to be broken off of my family heritage in the name of Jesus. I don't want this to continue in my bloodline ever again. I thank you, Lord, in Jesus' name!"

Take time to hear from Jesus, He will show you what you need to pray. Some sins are obvious but others He will reveal to you.

_____

_____

_____

_____

_____

_____

_____

Now see yourself giving Him all of your sorrows. Give Him the ashes of your life. Give Him the heaviness and depression that has hovered around you. Give Him all the "junk" in your life. He will gladly take it and replace it with His gifts.

- The beauty will come.

- The joy will come.

- His praise will forever be on your lips.

- Your life can be full of the fruits of God's Spirit.

Galatians 5:22-23 says, "But the fruit of the Spirit is love, joy, peace, longsuffering, kindness, goodness, faithfulness, gentleness, self-control. Against such there is no law."

This message is one that will not stop here on these pages. When you receive it, you will want to share your new-found freedom with others! When I was freed, I set out to learn all I could to help others. Before I knew it, training was available in more than one location and with many gifted people. God will not let us down when we seek Him for the answers. He knows what we need before we are even born. He always had a plan to restore us!

Philippians 4:4 says, "Rejoice in the Lord always. Again I will say, rejoice!"

Philippians 4: 6 says, "Be anxious for nothing, but in everything by prayer and supplication, with thanksgiving, let your requests be made known to God;"

Philippians 4:7 says, "And the peace of God, which surpasses all understanding, will guard your hearts and minds through Christ Jesus."

Philippians 4:8 says, "Finally, brethren, whatever things are true, whatever things are noble, whatever things are just, whatever things are pure, whatever things are lovely, whatever things are of good report, if there is any virtue and if there is anything praiseworthy—meditate on these things."

Philippians 4:13 says, "I can do all things through Christ who strengthens me."

This is a time for new beginnings so please take hold of what God has for you!

One of my favorite scriptures is found in Joel 2:25, "So I will restore to you the years that the swarming locust has eaten..."

I asked God to restore those years to me and I can honestly say He did!

I've been blessed with a wonderful husband for over thirty years. We've raised nine loving children, and we have fifteen beautiful grandchildren, three energetic step-grandchildren, and five little great-grandchildren. We are also blessed with a great son-in-law and daughter-in-law. If my life had been lost, I would not have been able to watch my beautiful children grow up, and I would have never known my wonderful grandchildren.

Our home is full of noise and laughter during the holidays!

Praise God, that He intervened in my life by revealing to me The Great Exchange, so that I am able to share my testimony with you!

Please use The Great Exchange in your own life and then pay it forward!

Chapter Sixteen

WHAT HAPPENS NEXT?

You may be asking, "What happens next?" After years of negative thinking and mind-boggling memories, you will be relieved to have a measure of freedom. This chapter will help you keep the healing and deliverance you have received. I hope you have taken the time to pray and listen to the truth. The beauty of the written page is that you can read and reflect on the truth over and over again.

As you can tell, the process I went through was a journey. Yours will be also. Think about a trip to the emergency room. You are always given "follow-up" instructions. You are instructed to check back with your own physician within a few days. Be thankful that Jesus is the Great Physician, and that we can come to Him over and over again as often as we like. A regular routine of seeking His will for our lives will continually change us.

In the previous chapter, I quoted Philippians 4:8, "Finally, brethren, whatever things are true, whatever things are noble, whatever things are just, whatever things are pure, whatever things are lovely, whatever things are of good report, if there is any virtue and if there is anything praiseworthy—meditate on these things." This verse could be titled "A Recipe for Good Mental Health." Notice the first thing it says you should focus on: TRUTH. When we focus on the truth, the lies are not able to come back to haunt us. When a lie begins to attack my mind, I say to myself, "Just wait a minute; I already know the truth about this." I refuse to let the lies come back to steal from my life.

There have been plenty of things that came my way to steal my self-worth. Sometimes harsh words make me feel like I'm not a good person, but I won't give those words power over me. I was once quick to agree with any degrading word spoken about me, but now I recognize it as a LIE.

Speak TRUTH to yourself!

Forgive the harsh words that have been spoken over you.

Most of us are our own worst enemy in this area. We do not need to beat ourselves up over our past, but we can learn from the past and make a good future. If you begin to practice living with TRUTH, you will feel different about yourself.

Earlier, I talked about seeing my self-image as "sleazy," even as a "whore." I don't care if you have been a prostitute, used as a slave, or victimized in ritual abuse, these are things that happened to you.

They Are Not Who You Are!

It was never God's intention for women and men to be used and abused.

Speak life over yourself. You have been given "Beauty for Ashes" (Isa.61). What I have shared with you will help you to become your own "life coach." The Spirit of God within you will always, always, reveal the truth to you.

There are other things that Philippians 4:8 tells us to hold our attention or thoughts on. I will break these down, one by one, according to Webster's Dictionary:

Noble: Having or showing high moral quality or ideals or greatness or character.

Just: Right, proper, fair, impartial, righteous, correct or true. (You will see that true or truth is in many of these definitions.)

Pure: Free from anything that is tainted or infects, flawless, free from sin or guilt, blameless.

Lovely: Beautiful, exquisite, morally and spiritually attractive, gracious.

Good Report: This one's not too hard for us to figure out. We need to listen to the good things that are being said and not the bad.

Virtue: Goodness, general moral excellence and right actions.

Praise-worthy: Simply *worthy of praise.*

These are the things that the Lord wants us to concentrate on, to think on, to fill our minds with, and to fill our hearts with.

There have been times in my life when I decided to make a list of everything for which I had to be thankful. I didn't decide to do it because I was so overcome by joy and thankfulness that I had to write it down on paper. I made the list because the things in life that were going on around me looked so hopeless and depressing that I had to seek TRUTH. When I began to make the list, I did not have a thankful heart, and I could barely come up with anything. As I wrote, little by little the list grew and grew.

I don't care how bad things seem, if we focus on the goodness of God and the truth, our dark clouds begin to roll away. I remember a time when my circumstances seemed impossible, but God turned them around in my favor. Over and over again, my needs have been met. Remember that light expels darkness!

We have a choice to look deep into the darkness and allow our lives to be overcome by despair. We also have a choice to look and listen to truth and have thankful hearts.

I chose TRUTH!

In the last chapter, you began to write down the things you believed were being shown to you. Continue to keep a notebook or journal of your thoughts and prayers. This is an outline of a prescription for being healthy and whole, emotionally and spiritually, as well as physically at times. (You may have heard someone say, "You will worry yourself to death." Stress does cause sickness and disease.)

As long as we live in this world, we will be hurt by people. They may or may not mean to, but it will happen. You will have plenty of chances to forgive. The night "Heaven touched Earth" for me was just the beginning. We are much like plants in a garden that need to be tended to. The young, tender shoots need water, good soil, and sunlight. The weeds need to be plucked away.

You will need to put good things into your life if you want the good fruit to come out of it. Surround yourself with good, positive people. Find friends who are wanting to grow in Christ. Seek out someone with whom you can share your new-found freedom. There are many good Bible-believing churches where you can make friends and become part of a support group. Read God's Word and it will help you find the truth for your life. God's love is contagious, share it wherever you go. Look up, head held high, and be proud of who God made you to be.

Revelations 12:11 says, "And they overcame him by the blood of the Lamb and by the word of their testimony..."

When I tell my story, it reminds me of God's love for me. It shows me that He will never leave me and has always had a plan for my life. Your own testimony is the story of the good things God has done in your life. It is the story of your healing and deliverance. Your story is powerful. Your story needs to touch someone else. The truth of what God has done for you will not only strengthen them, but it will continually strengthen you and bring you more deliverance. Share it! God's love flows in you.

What Are Your Sugar Cubes?!

We have all used them. Little things that fill our lives to take away the pain. They soothe us quickly but vanish just as quickly, leaving us empty. They are like junk food void of the precious nutrition our bodies need. It's like counterfeit dollars that spend quickly but have no real value at all. Something has filled the hollow places in your heart. For thousands it is drugs and alcohol. Whatever it is, I believe you have recognized it as you read this book. The TRUTH is, whatever SUGAR CUBE you have savored as it melted in your mouth, was a substitute for the healing balm that Jesus has for you. Let us see our SUGAR CUBES like bread crumbs that lead us, like Hansel and Gretel, along the path to home. So, take that full bowl and drop those things beneath your feet. THEY HAVE NOT MADE YOU STRONG so why not use them? Stand on them to shout your freedom to all who will listen. Through our weakness He has made us strong.

What WERE your SUGAR CUBES?!!!

_____

_____

_____

I am forever rejoicing to hear of the lives God has set free. If you have a testimony that you would like to share with me, you may write me at:

L. G. Gibson
PO Box 285
Wilkesboro, NC 28697
www.throughtearsandsugarcubes.org

If you enjoyed this book, please post a review of it where you purchased it. Thank you in advance.

Minnie's Pecan Crispy Cookies

This is the cookie recipe promised from Chapter One. Make some new memories and some great cookies!

Preheat oven to 350. Cooking time 10-15 minutes. Makes 5 dozen.

½ cup shortening (Crisco)
½ cup butter
2 ½ cups of firmly packed brown sugar
2 eggs beaten

Cream together the first ingredients and beat well

2 ½ cups plain flour
½ t soda
½ t salt

Blend together.

Add all dry ingredients to creamed mixture

1 cup chopped Pecans

Stir in nuts

Drop from a teaspoon onto cookie sheet

Bake and enjoy!

This is dedicated to a precious woman of God, my Grandmother, Minnie Lee Pender.

L. G. Gibson

L.G. Gibson is a licensed and ordained minister with over thirty-five years of experience. As a survivor of sexual abuse herself, she has spent countless hours focusing her efforts on helping others heal from the trauma of abuse as a teacher, faith-based mentor, crisis intervention counselor, public speaker, and a missionary to seven countries. She is currently raising her ninth child and was a foster parent of four additional children. She resides in North Carolina with her husband, Russell.

Testimonials for
Through Tears and Sugar Cubes

"L.G. Gibson speaks with great compassion, sensitivity and authority on the subjects of abuse and subsequent healing. With her typical Southern Style, Linda warms the hearts of her readers, paving the way for the Holy Spirit to work His healing miracles in the deep, unseen places of the heart. Her story is real, and her desire to glorify her Heavenly Father in all things shines through."

Julie Appleyard, co-founder of ANOTHEN, Author of *Boardroom of the Inner Man*

"I encourage everyone who desires to experience the 'free indeed' Jesus said He came to give to apply the information presented in this book to their own life experiences and begin living the abundant, happy and joyous life Jesus paid for you to live. It is never too late to begin again!"

Diana Sykes, Author

"She has truly helped me with issues that I had dealt with for most of my life. The way the Holy Spirit ministers through her is just so gentle but powerful... life changing. She carries so much of Jesus love and compassion. I love her!"

Joy Kirk, Business Owner and Minister

"I received freedom from a life of self-hatred, self-condemnation, and poor body image that had led to an eating disorder. I can say that through the tools and strategies found in this book, I learned not only to hear God's voice, but to see myself through His lens."

Amanda

"As I read this book, my eyes were opened. My heart is no longer heavy with sadness or anger toward the people who have hurt me. I am forever changed because of this book."

Amber